D0461862

DRINKING
SMOKING &
SCREWING

DRINKING
SMOKING &
SCREWING

Great Writers on Good Times

Edited by Sara Nicklès
Introduction by Bob Shacochis

CHRONICLE BOOKS

SAN FRANCISCO

Library of Congress Cataloging-in-Publication Data

Drinking, Smoking, and Screwing: Great Writers on Good Times edited by Sara Nicklès; introduction by Bob Shacochis
p. cm. ISBN 0-8118-0784-3 (pb) 1. American literature—20th century
2. Drinking customs—Literary collections 3. Sex customs—Literary collections 4. Smoking—Literary collections
I. Nicklès, Sara. PS509.D74 1994 810.8'0355—dc20
94-9336
CIP

Cover design: Adrian Morgan at Red Letter
Book design: Kristin Beckstoffer

Distributed in Canada by Raincoast Books,
8680 Cambie Street, Vancouver, B.C. V6P 6M9

10 9 8 7 6 5 4 3

Chronicle Books
275 Fifth Street
San Francisco, CA 94103

For Louis Charles Nicklès and Serge Gainsbourg,
pour leurs vices enthousiastes.

TABLE OF CONTENTS

I asked my friend, "What are your three favorite pleasures in life?" and she replied, "A martini before and a cigarette after."

—Unknown

INTRODUCTION

Bob Shacochis

Among the things that make life worth living for some of us wretched souls is the kind of bad—though not evil—behavior that can be roughly characterized as sin. Yet, heaven knows, these days sin—however stylish and satisfying, and despite its generous contribution to the overall *texture* of that state of grace known as being alive—has fallen into disrepute. Since only a fool would defend it, I volunteered, understanding of course that I would be in good company.

I've passed my HIV blood test, my most recent chest X ray reveals no horrific shadow-clump of cells, and my designated driver is out at curbside, awaiting my tipsy arrival. I know I'm not going to live forever, and neither are you, but until my furlough here on earth is revoked, I should like to elbow aside the established pieties and raise my martini glass in salute to the mortal arts of pleasure. Specifically, drinking, smoking, and screwing—those much-maligned but eternally seductive temptations of the flesh, those impetuous jockeys of the spirit. Vice, after all, is not wholly without virtue and, like virtue, must sometimes settle for being its own reward. Nor has vice lacked its advocates over the years (though a great many of them now appear to be dead or in retreat). If you're a paragon of self-control and moral clarity, and perhaps think that a habit as pernicious as smoking has nothing in its dossier to recommend it, untuck your joie de vivre from its fetal ball for a moment and listen to Don Marquis's "Preface to a

Book of Cigarette Papers," which appeared in 1919, a halcyon year for the mystique of misbehaving:

All that is romantic and literary and spiritual in us holds by the cigarette. When we die and are purged of all the heavy flesh that holds us down, our soul, we hope, will roll and smoke cigarettes along with Buck the romantic and lying cowboy and Ariel and [R. L.] Stevenson and Benvenuto Cellini and Jack Hamlin. We have never been the person on earth we should like to be; circumstances have always tied us to the staid and commonplace and respectable; but when we become an angel we hope to be right devilish at times. And that is an idea that some one should work out—Hell as a place of reward for Puritans.

On the other hand, in an age of co-dependency, self-congratulatory illiteracy, and the crusade for correctness, what's the point in lighting up? Will today's audience, reading Corey Ford's "The Office Party," published in 1951, even know that rye is also a whiskey and not just a bread? (What they will understand, certainly, is that the merrymaking Ford describes is strictly verboten in the contemporary workplace.)

I remember—at least I think I do, it's all rather murky—when I indeed *was* the person I wanted to be, when it was customary for me to drink, smoke, and (attempt to) screw with liberal abandon, put my heart and soul into it. As a bon vivant and rascal, I once showed great promise; apparently I was precocious, I had a future in decadence. But then came the '80s and, even worse, the '90s, and the zealous reformation of the liberated counterculture into a priggish, middle-aged nation of naggers and health harpies. We didn't just become our parents, we became our parents *with a vengeance,* determined to fashion an aggressively sanitized world that held about as much appeal for us backsliders as a date with a coed from Antioch. Can I stand in this room with you? Can I breathe your air? Can I touch your hair? How about your anus?

For reasons I have yet to fathom, in the new world order, so that we might lead better, more fruitful and lasting lives, we are all now entitled to be utterly sick and tired of one another. Fran Lebowitz, in her visionary essay "When Smoke Gets in Your Eyes ... Shut Them," saw it coming: "Being offended is that natural consequence of leaving one's home. I do not like after-shave lotion, adults who roller-skate, children who speak French, or anyone who is unduly tan," wrote Lebowitz in 1977. "In private I avoid such people; in public they have the run of the place. I stay at home as much as possible, and so should they. When it is necessary, however, to go out of the house, they must be prepared, as I am, to deal with the unpleasant personal habits of others. That is what 'public' means. If you can't stand the heat, get back in the kitchen."

Like myself, Lebowitz once thought that smoking, drinking, and screwing were the entire point of being an adult. They made growing up, she said, genuinely worthwhile. Now we both realize that the real point in growing up is to hire lawyers and engage in litigation. We both made the mistake of imagining that the personal was, well, a personal matter, rather than somebody else's political agenda. Sometime during the past ten years things changed. It no longer makes sense whether you keep to yourself or not: If you are doing something in your own kitchen that pisses off the surgeon general you are, ipso facto, a public nuisance.

Somehow, the nation allowed propriety and good sense to become hyper-inflated commodities. While truth became relative, peccadilloes began to sag with the weight of the absolute, and suddenly the mystery of personality was a victim of realpolitik. Evidence was presented to suggest that sins against one's self were, in effect, offensive—in other words, sins unconscionably committed against one's neighbor, who roamed audaciously through one's backyard aiming a video camera. Drinkers, smokers, and fornicators were hence transformed—if you enjoy vulgar imagery (and I know plenty of you still do)—into turds battling upcurrent against the purified, utopian flow of the self-improved mainstream. Decent people could finally relax about the impending fall of the American Empire.

> Then the first thing will be to establish a censorship of the writers of fiction, and let the censors receive any tale of fiction which is good, and reject the bad; and we will desire mothers and nurses to tell their children the authorized ones only.
>
> —Plato, *The Republic*

Until March 21, 1966, when a lawyer named Charles Rembar successfully defended before the Supreme Court the literary merit of three banned books—*Lady Chatterley's Lover, Tropic of Cancer,* and *Fanny Hill*—if you wrote, published, or sold a book that had the potential to stir up "genital commotion" in a reader, there was a pretty good chance you'd end up in jail. Which is what happened in 1930 to a bookseller who sold Theodore Dreiser's allegedly "lewd and obscene" novel *An American Tragedy.* The enlightened state of New York prosecuted Edmund Wilson in the 1940s for *Memoirs of Hecate County.* In the 1950s, the U.S. Customs Service banned Henry Miller's *Tropics,* and the city of Boston banned almost everything else.

Many of the works excerpted here were widely considered to be scandalous and subversive when they were first published—Nabokov's *Lolita,* Mary McCarthy's *The Group,* Donleavy's *The Ginger Man.* Many of the writers were accused of "blackening," so to speak, that mainstay of genteel literature, the comedy of manners. Here were the Laureates of Sin, dragging their shocking, sordid esthetics of corruption into the drawing room. And as likely as not, sniggering about it.

My timing, and the timing of this book, is perhaps way off here, given the intensified backlash against some of our more popular blue-chip transgressions: fatal addiction, vile intemperance, and deplorable lust. One struggles to keep pace with the moral conventions du jour as the menu evolves, undergoes erasure, and recycles. Say, is Catherine MacKinnon really the reincarnation of Anthony Comstock or what? "Anything that's your heart's desire," Eve Babitz noted early in the game, "sooner or later turns into a sin."

But when the pleasures of being a mere mortal become too perilous for pursuit, is it possible we've outgrown growing up? Is it possible, to paraphrase Oscar Wilde, that disobedience, in the eyes of anyone who has read history, is no longer man's original virtue?

The Marquis de Sade claimed, rightly, that his was the work of a moralist. Oscar Wilde insisted that both vice and virtue are equally irreplaceable materials for art. Cynthia Ozick called storytellers and novelists a "stewpot of bad habits" who "enter the demonic as a matter of course," all in the service of rapture. "You can't write out of fear of offending anybody," John Updike recently told an interviewer, probably for the umpteenth time. "You have to push your vision." The collective wisdom of all these points of view is crystallized in a single line from Jean Paulhan's preface to the infamous *Story of O:* "Dangerous books are those that restore us to our natural state of danger."

DRINKING, SMOKING & SCREWING

It is the role of the social and cultural reformer to brick over that danger with layer upon layer of prophylaxis. The hazards of existence, however, can't be removed, they can only be muffled or obscured. Yet a concealed danger has a much greater potential for damage than one that has been dragged out into the light, posted with warning signs and, perhaps, even befriended. I think it is for this reason that the writer has a special contract with sin and society, a license granted to conduct all manner of moral investigations into the labyrinth of human nature, a safe pass issued for the exploration of the volatile dichotomy between the body and the soul. When self-control becomes self-denial, the writer asks, what is gained, and what is lost? Will desire always play the villain in the human drama? Are our sexual awakenings destined to be gates to disaster, or is there really such a thing as a Zipless Fuck? What are the secrets of moderation, and who invented the cocktail anyway?

The inescapable fact is that what you bind yourself to, either by passion, love, or duty, is going to be the end of you, one way or the other. It's true that the Marlboro Man is stone dead of lung cancer, regretting the countless small, harsh but transcendent moments of pleasure he inhaled with his tobacco. And it is true that drinking is no longer generally considered to be an upright profession, and it is outrageously true that the poets' linkage of sex and death is particularly apropos to our times, seeing as how we now kill each other with our genitals at a much more alarming rate than we do with our guns.

Frankly though, I doubt that anyone's ever pleased by the form their death takes. (And what about the Jamaican proverb: A man condemned to hang can't drown?) For the "prim marms of puritanism" it's all about dying, isn't it? If Charles Darwin was correct, smokers, drinkers, and libertines are doing the species a favor, accelerating the biological quest for perfection.

But spiritual quests aren't so simple, and sometimes they lure the seeker into smoky barrooms and the arms of an unexpected lover. Hot damn! Or maybe not. It's futile, I suppose, to defend smoking, drinking, and fucking. Nevertheless, not to defend smokers, drinkers, and fuckers would be a terrible mistake. Who wants to live in a world without them, without their libidinous hunger, without their exalted obsessions? They take the joy and sometimes the pain of living to the very edge and shout back instructions, dire caveats, titillating weather reports. They inspire great writing and bring a reader's blood to the boiling point. Without them, the world might be simple and clean, but it wouldn't be deliciously, fascinatingly, pathetically human, would it?

Nor would it be much fun.

YOU WERE PERFECTLY FINE

Dorothy Parker

The pale young man eased himself carefully into the low chair, and rolled his head to the side, so that the cool chintz comforted his cheek and temple.

"Oh, dear," he said. "Oh, dear, oh, dear, oh, dear. Oh."

The clear-eyed girl, sitting light and erect on the couch, smiled brightly at him.

"Not feeling so well today?" she said.

"Oh, I'm great," he said. "Corking, I am. Know what time I got up? Four o'clock this afternoon, sharp. I kept trying to make it, and every time I took my head off the pillow, it would roll under the bed. This isn't my head I've got on now. I think this is something that used to belong to Walt Whitman. Oh, dear, oh, dear, oh, dear."

"Do you think maybe a drink would make you feel better?" she said.

"The hair of the mastiff that bit me?" he said. "Oh, no, thank you. Please never speak of anything like that again. I'm through. I'm all, all through. Look at that hand; steady as a humming-bird. Tell me, was I very terrible last night?"

"Oh, goodness," she said, "everybody was feeling pretty high. You were all right."

"Yeah," he said. "I must have been dandy. Is everybody sore at me?"

"Good heavens, no," she said. "Everyone thought you were terribly funny. Of course, Jim Pierson was a little stuffy, there, for a minute at dinner. But people sort of held him back in his chair, and got him calmed down. I don't think anybody at the other tables noticed it at all. Hardly anybody."

"He was going to sock me?" he said. "Oh, Lord. What did I do to him?"

"Why, you didn't do a thing," she said. "You were perfectly fine. But you know how silly Jim gets, when he thinks anybody is making too much fuss over Elinor."

"Was I making a pass at Elinor?" he said. "Did I do that?"

"Of course you didn't," she said. "You were only fooling, that's all. She thought you were awfully amusing. She was having a marvelous time. She only got a little tiny bit annoyed just once, when you poured the clam-juice down her back."

"My God," he said. "Clam-juice down that back. And every vertebra a little Cabot. Dear God. What'll I ever do?"

"Oh, she'll be all right," she said. "Just send her some flowers, or something. Don't worry about it. It isn't anything."

"No, I won't worry," he said. "I haven't got a care in the world. I'm sitting pretty. Oh, dear, oh, dear. Did I do any other fascinating tricks at dinner?"

"You were fine," she said. "Don't be so foolish about it. Everybody was crazy about you. The maître d'hôtel was a little worried because you wouldn't stop singing, but he really didn't mind. All he said was, he was afraid they'd close the place again, if there was so much noise. But he didn't care a bit, himself. I think he loved seeing you have such a good time. Oh, you were just singing away, there, for about an hour. It wasn't so terribly loud, at all."

"So I sang," he said. "That must have been a treat. I sang."

"Don't you remember?" she said. "You just sang one song after another. Everybody in the place was listening. They loved it. Only you kept insisting that you wanted to sing some song about some kind of fusiliers or other, and everybody kept shushing you, and you'd keep trying to start it again. You were wonderful. We were all trying to make you stop singing for a minute, and eat something, but you wouldn't hear of it. My, you were funny."

"Didn't I eat any dinner?" he said.

"Oh, not a thing," she said. "Every time the waiter would offer you something, you'd give it right back to him, because you said that he was your long-lost brother, changed in the cradle by a gypsy band, and that anything you had was his. You had him simply roaring at you."

"I bet I did," he said. "I bet I was comical. Society's Pet, I must have been. And what happened then, after my overwhelming success with the waiter?"

"Why, nothing much," she said. "You took a sort of dislike to some old man with white hair, sitting across the room, because you didn't like his necktie and you wanted to tell him about it. But we got you out, before he got really mad."

"Oh, we got out," he said. "Did I walk?"

"Walk! Of course you did," she said. "You were absolutely all right. There was that nasty stretch of ice on the sidewalk, and you did sit down awfully hard, you poor dear. But good heavens, that might have happened to anybody."

"Oh, sure," he said. "Louisa Alcott or anybody. So I fell down on the sidewalk. That would explain what's the matter with my—Yes. I see. And then what, if you don't mind?"

"Ah, now, Peter!" she said. "You can't sit there and say you don't remember what happened after that! I did think that maybe you were just a little tight at dinner—oh, you were perfectly all right, and all that, but I did know you were feeling pretty gay. But you were so serious, from the time you fell down—I never knew you to be that way. Don't you know, how you told me I had never seen your real self before? Oh, Peter, I just couldn't bear it, if you didn't remember that lovely long ride we took together in the taxi! Please, you do remember that, don't you? I think it would simply kill me, if you didn't."

"Oh, yes," he said. "Riding in the taxi. Oh, yes, sure. Pretty long ride, hmm?"

"Round and round and round the park," she said. "Oh, and the trees were shining so in the moonlight. And you said you never knew before that you really had a soul."

"Yes," he said. "I said that. That was me."

"You said such lovely, lovely things," she said. "And I'd never known, all this time, how you had been feeling about me, and I'd never dared to let you see how I felt about you. And then last night—oh, Peter dear, I think that taxi ride was the most important thing that ever happened to us in our lives."

"Yes," he said. "I guess it must have been."

"And we're going to be so happy," she said. "Oh, I just want to tell everybody! But I don't know—I think maybe it would be sweeter to keep it all to ourselves."

"I think it would be," he said.

"Isn't it lovely?" she said.

"Yes," he said. "Great."

"Lovely!" she said.

"Look here," he said, "do you mind if I have a drink? I mean, just medicinally, you know. I'm off the stuff for life, so help me. But I think I feel a collapse coming on."

"Oh, I think it would do you good," she said. "You poor boy, it's a shame you feel so awful. I'll go make you a whisky and soda."

"Honestly," he said, "I don't see how you could ever want to speak to me again, after I made such a fool of myself, last night. I think I'd better go join a monastery in Tibet."

"You crazy idiot!" she said. "As if I could ever let you go away now! Stop talking like that. You were perfectly fine."

She jumped up from the couch, kissed him quickly on the forehead, and ran out of the room.

The pale young man looked after her and shook his head long and slowly, then dropped it in his damp and trembling hands.

"Oh, dear," he said. "Oh, dear, oh, dear, oh, dear."

[1928]

COLLEGE GIRLS

Spalding Gray

I was a virgin when I entered college. Freshman year I was at a party, and my friend Stubbs came up to me and said, "You see that girl? Her name's Sandy, and she goes down. And I'm going to go down with her before the night's over." I thought I'd try to beat him out. I went up to her and said, "Hi Sandy, my name's Spud and I hear you go down." We spent the night together. I began by licking her breasts. She said, "Who do you think I am, your mother?" Then we had intercourse and I came in about 30 seconds. I ended up lying there for the rest of the night staring up at the ceiling, which wasn't all that bad because it was one of those ceilings in old Boston houses painted with little cherubs flying through the clouds, and it was something to look at. The only bad thing about it was that Zapata, the Latin lover from Cuba, was making love to his girlfriend right on the other side of a partition that didn't go all the way up to the ceiling. They really carried on. I had heard stories about Zapata. I had heard that he had made his girlfriend take a nylon stocking, tie it in little knots, and fold it up and stick it up his ass; then, while she was giving him a blow job, just before he was going to come, she tore it out. I had *that* to contend with.

I hadn't gotten much sleep at all, and in the morning I just wanted to get out of there. I didn't know the right thing to do or the wrong thing, even. Zapata was calling out, over the partition, "Hey, nothing like starting the morning with a little good loving," in his Spanish accent. His brother Aroozoo was the same. I was over at his apartment once and Aroozoo had been in bed with his girl-friend for three days and three nights, and they hadn't washed any of the dishes. Zapata started in on them in Spanish about the dishes and Aroozoo got up and said, "I'll wash the dishes" and took them and threw them out in the hall, smashed every one of them, and said, "There, they're done."

So Sandy decided to bring me back to her apartment for breakfast. I didn't want to go, I had no appetite at all. And she served me eggs, baked. I'd never had baked eggs before. She baked them in the oven and after I had the baked eggs, I hightailed it out of there, fast. I went back to my dorm room and rolled around on the floor, praying to God to forgive me and swearing I'd never do it again. After that, when I saw Sandy in the halls of Emerson College, I'd run for the men's room, and I never went after another girl my whole freshman year.

My sophomore year, I was allowed to move out of the dorms and get my own place. I rented an apartment like a little house in an alley behind two buildings on Newbury Street. The arrangement was that I would pay only $30 a month for this little alley bunker with window bars, provided I swept the halls and emptied the trash in the two buildings. That wasn't a bad job, except for having to pick up the flaky pieces of shell from the hard-boiled eggs of Mrs. Fletcher, the real estate lady. What was worse was that my apartment was in the alley, and those back alleys in Boston were alive with rats. They would squeal and carry on like kittens outside my door at dusk. At night when I'd come home, I would clap my hands to get them out of the way. My friends called the place "Rat Alley," and girls would rarely visit.

Once a baby rat had crawled into a garbage pail and was stuck in there, just squealing and jumping up on the side. I didn't have the heart to kill or the mind to set it free.

Some girls did stay over, but I don't remember any sexual intercourse. In fact, there was no intercourse at all. One time I lay down on Adele Schreck when we were both naked and I caught crabs. I treated it like a major venereal disease. I went to a private doctor and he prescribed my first A-200 crab lice remover.

Once Monica Moran showed up at the Newbury Street apartment. I knew Monica from Fitchton Academy, where she had chosen me to be her boyfriend during our senior year. I didn't say yes and I didn't say no, until one cold winter night she snuck out of her dorm and came knocking on my fire escape door. I had a single room senior year at Fitchton. It was actually more like a closet than a room, and it had a door that led right out onto the fire escape. I couldn't imagine who'd be out there at that time of night. I opened my door and let Monica sit on the edge of the bed. She told me she'd come to give her virginity away. I had just been reading Freud for the first time—his essay on narcissism. I said, "Monica, do you know what a narcissist is?" And she said, "Of course." I said, "Well, I think I am one, that's why I can't respond to you." We had a good talk anyway.

So here was Monica in Boston. She came to visit me in Rat Alley and she was still a virgin. And I still didn't respond. Then she went off to Cambridge to lose her cherry with some guy and came back to tell me she wasn't a virgin anymore and that she had done it just for me. I tried to go to bed with her this time, with the rats squealing outside. At first I felt nothing, so I decided to get very drunk. Then I felt nothing even more. Finally,

I just threw up. So Monica gave up on me as a lover and we became friends.

My junior year I moved up in the world. I got a furnished room on Marlborough Street. It was much more elegant and I felt like I was living in London. I began to read all the existentialists, drink Chivas Regal, and eat sunflower seeds. Some girls came to visit me there, but none that I was really attracted to.

One time Tammy Mahoney, an old girlfriend of Felix Quinn's, looked me up. I had met her once at his place in New York. After she had broken up with Felix she got married and moved to Hadley, Massachusetts. Her husband turned out to be a wife abuser and beat her up. When she got out of the hospital she fled to Boston and sought me out. Tammy was cute and sassy, with small breasts. I had no trouble looking at her nude body; it was like a sweet little nut. But getting close enough to touch her was a whole other thing. It was like a steeplechase.

She began by reading Camus's "The Myth of Sisyphus," and soon I'd get her down to the buff. She baited me into chasing her as she leapt over the armchair and pranced along the back of the couch. But I never caught up with her. Even if I had, I don't think I'd have known what to do. Then she'd reread "The Myth of Sisyphus" naked, by candlelight. Or sometimes we'd go to a Bergman movie and come home depressed, drink some scotch and eat some sunflower seeds, and go to sleep in separate beds. After reading "The Myth of Sisyphus" a few more times, Tammy would go back to Hadley to get beat up.

Then Melanie Truscott came into my life. She was 17, a freshman at Emerson, and a model for *Seventeen* magazine. She was tall, blond, and thin, with hardly any breasts. Her breasts were so small she wouldn't take off her bra, and I didn't insist. When we made love, she'd always make a lot of noise, and afterward she'd ask me why I was so quiet. She told me her last boyfriend made a lot of noise when he came. I was always under the impression it was a sign of good sex to laugh a lot like Henry VIII—you know, "Ho ho ho ho ho" and all that, like a sexy Santa Claus, but no laughter was coming, not even an ounce.

But we were laughing a lot outside of bed. I used to play practical jokes on Melanie. I was working as a kitchen boy at the Katie Gibbs Secretarial School in Boston. If you worked at Katie Gibbs you were not allowed to date any of the girls-women, women-girls there at all. That was fine with me; it left me feeling totally free. I felt like a good castrato. I felt more creative because I didn't feel as though I was being led around by my balls. I could make jokes and say whatever came into my mind. Like when I was scraping their plates at the garbage wagon, I'd say, "What are you throwing your roast beef away for?" (Thursdays we'd have roast beef.) "Think of all the starving people in the world!" And they'd say, "We pay for it, we do what we want with it." So on Thursdays all this roast beef would go into the garbage disposal, which we called "The Pig," to be ground up and sent out to the Charles River, so the fish were really eating well out there. They were probably hanging around that particular drainage pipe. And on Fridays they'd serve fish, and every Friday their sisters and brothers would come out there ground up. We would have terrific fish on Friday, scrod or cod, well-done. Well-baked. Baked well. Real well. With a little paprika on the top.

And I got on well with the women there, the Irish Catholic women, and all the cooks, until John F. Kennedy was shot and I overreacted a little bit. I came in when they were all weeping in the corner and I went, "Come on, what's going on? Don't let a little shooting hold up the dinner." And it took some time to get them back as friends.

The cooks used to give me leftover pea soup, that was my favorite, to take home in a half-gallon milk carton. It'd be cold and gray-looking when you took it out, but when you reheated it, it was fine. One day I was going to heat some up for Melanie and I stuck my arm into the carton, up to the elbow, to scoop out some soup. I looked down and there were globs of cold, gray pea soup hanging off my arm, and I went, "Ah, ah, ah, ahchew! Oh, Melanie look! I sneezed my brains out all over my—" "Oh, no!" she screamed, "not right before dinner." I didn't know a lot of the time who was fooling whom. For instance, once I went down to the Charles River. I was a sun worshiper, and I wanted to lie in the sun there. When I came back, I opened the refrigerator and peeled the skin off some overcooked chicken that was all black and bubbly. I unbuttoned my shirt and put it on my shoulder. Then I said, "Oh, Melanie, Melanie, I've got a bad burn. I got too much sun. Give me a little cream rub, please." And she pulled open my shirt and screamed.

When I was in college, I was always afraid to urinate when girls were around. I was afraid to pee directly into the toilet bowl because I had the feeling that girls judged the size of your cock by the sound of the flow, and I didn't want any kind of judgment going on. So I would always pee on the inside of the bowl and sometimes it would go a little over the edge. But with Melanie, I would take two big empty grapefruit juice bottles, fill them with water and dump them one at a time, very slowly into the toilet bowl. This would go on for five minutes while she was outside, screaming with laughter.

Somewhere along the line, I think Melanie felt I wasn't

paying enough attention to her, that I was too self-absorbed. So she staged a fake rape scene in order to get my attention. To this day, I think it was fake. I was studying theater at the time, and I knew bad acting when I saw it. A mutual friend of Melanie's and mine came rushing into my room on Marlborough Street one day and said, "Oh listen, listen. I'm really sorry. I just got overtaken with lust and accidentally raped Melanie. You've got to forgive me." I said, "Oh, that's all right, Danny. I forgive you." We talked for a while. Shortly after he left, Melanie came running in, and something about her timing made me think she'd been hiding just outside the door all the time. She threw herself on the bed and started screaming, "Danny raped me!" I said, "Oh, gee. That's too bad. Is there anything I can do to help?"

Well, we broke up shortly after that. And when we were breaking up she told me that she had faked all her climaxes. Now, I didn't mind that so much as the idea that she might have been faking the laughter over the chicken, the grapefruit jars, and the pea soup.

My senior year I moved into an apartment on Beacon Street. I loved that apartment. It was so simple and empty that it made me feel like a Zen monk. There was a small fireplace, two straight-back chairs, and a single mattress in the corner on the floor. There was a hot plate and a refrigerator, but no kitchen table, so I ate the leftover food I brought home from Katie Gibbs standing up.

Irena Cleveland was one of the first black girls I'd ever known, and it was at this time that I almost got involved with her. She was a virgin and very beautiful. I had never been involved with a black girl before, and I was titillated and confused. On our first date, she came over to my apartment and we got very high on Gallo sherry. Then I got out my new Ouija Board and we began to play. Irena and I were asking the regular questions about when the world was going to end, how many children we would have, and what spirits out there had any important messages for us, when at last the board spelled out I-R-E-N-A. Irena and I asked the board what about Irena, and it spelled out F-U-C-K-H-E-R-A-N-D-F-I-N-D-O-U-T. We both leaned back and laughed. I was sure neither of us were manipulating the board. We were both too innocent and neither would have talked like that. Well, I just turned to Irena and blushed. We got into bed, fully dressed, and I just laid down beside her. Then I put my arm around her and she burst into tears. When I asked her what was wrong, she said that her mother had been encouraging her to lose her virginity, but she didn't know how. Also, she wasn't sure that she really wanted to before she got married.

This was during the Cuban missile crisis, when, after Kennedy's speech, all the Emerson College girls ran out of the dorms, screaming, "Take me. I don't want to die a virgin! Please, take me!" After that I kept having these obsessive fantasies about how I would go to the girl's dorm all dressed in white lace, with three eunuch slaves carrying bull whips. And I'd just go from room to room deflowering all these flowers.

But Irena Cleveland wasn't one of them. Irena thought she wanted to be a virgin when she got married, so we just spent the night sitting around, drinking sherry, and listening to the last movement of Beethoven's Ninth, over and over again.

Kit Tobin was a student at the University of New Hampshire, and I thought that would be a little safer because she could only hitchhike down to see me on weekends. And since I was involved in a theater production, rehearsing for Molière's *The Misanthrope,* I had a perfect excuse to make her come to me. We had a great relationship, except that she didn't like fish. That was a problem, because every Friday when she arrived from Amherst, I would serve her the leftover fish I brought home from work. I still didn't have any chairs, so we would eat standing up. I was too cheap to take her out. Each Friday she'd come down and I'd serve her a little leftover fish with garlic, a little leftover fish with curry, a little leftover fish with tomato, until one Friday she came down to visit and said, "Oh, God. Not fish again," and started throwing up. She threw up all night long.

The next weekend Kit called me from Amherst and said that she wanted to talk, and could she come to my parents' house in Barrington over Christmas vacation. I said yes. When she got down there she said, "I met someone in Amherst who gives me more." I didn't know more of *what.* I didn't ask. Then she said, "I'm going to be seeing him, and I have to tell you something we did together, but I don't want you to tell anyone." I said, "I won't." And she said, "We went to a barn, a bunch of us, outside Amherst, and we smoked marijuana together."

So she left. I went indoors, drank about a fifth of vodka and got very drunk. I thought, I've got to go to the theater. This is the only recourse, I will go see *The Caretaker* at the Trinity Square Playhouse in Providence. I went to ask my parents for the keys to the car and my mother said, "What's wrong, dear?" And I burst into tears and said, "I've lost Kit. I'll *never* find anyone like her again." And my mother said, "Well, that's what you said about the last one, dear." I don't remember ever saying that. They gave me the keys to the car and I drove off to Providence. The road was like a roller coaster, and every five minutes I was opening the door and vomiting my guts out. The next day I had such a hangover I felt like I was going to die. But I loved the play. It was then that I made up my mind. No more booze, no more love, no more girlfriends. I was going to devote my life to the stage.

Now that I wasn't drinking at night, I was much more aware of the Beacon Street noise. I began to close down. It began quite simply with plugging my ears. I did this with wet toilet paper. I would take the toilet paper and run it under warm water. Then I would shape it into two wads, smear a little Jergen's hand cream on each of them, and fit them into my ears.

But the toilet paper wasn't enough. I still felt assaulted by sound. I designed three soundproof shutters for the windows in my apartment. I cut them out of plywood and backed them with fiberglass insulation. Then at night I put the shutters up and plugged my ears with the wet toilet paper.

One morning I just decided to leave them up. The Back Bay Community Association sent me a letter requesting that I take the shutters down. I didn't. Next they sent a representative who looked like T. S. Eliot knocking at my door. When I asked him what was wrong, he said that from the street, the external insulation on the shutters made my apartment look like a construction site, so would I please take them down. I didn't.

About this time I dreamt I had lost my testicles. Either they had dropped off or someone had cut them off with a scissors, I don't know which. I was searching for them on a football field. I think it was Victory Field in Barrington, Rhode Island. At last I found my balls behind the seats, just hanging there from the bottom of the bleachers.

I went to the student psychiatric clinic to have a little talk with the therapist there. After listening to me for about half an hour he said, "You are suffering from a drawn-out case of postadolescence." He talked about how nowadays that sort of thing could go on until you were 40. Thinking I should get a second opinion, I consulted a therapist at Mass. General. After about 20 minutes, he stopped me and said, "You're just a big existential garbage pail. Go home and relax."

Then I met Adriana Alexis Glick, the first sensual love of my life. She was brunette and beautiful. She was from the upper West Side of New York City, and she was going to Emerson College. We had a very romantic relationship. I had a fireplace, a working fireplace, but I was too cheap to buy firewood. So after we struck *The Misanthrope* set, I had the crew bring it over and put it in the corner of my apartment. It was piled almost to the ceiling. I burned *The Misanthrope* set while we lay naked on this mattress in front of the fireplace, sipping sparkling rosé out of matching hollow-stemmed champagne glasses and listening to the Fantasia on "Greensleeves." The fire would be burning and we'd be sipping and we'd be kissing, having a little sex and a lot of petting. Once she tried to suck my cock. I said, "What are you doing?" And she said, "Well, I just wanted to kiss it, you know." After we made love, I would ask her to go home so that I could be alone and suffer for the same amount of time that I had had pleasure with her. And I would put on some Berlioz and drink another bottle of wine and I would suffer, and I would sleep alone.

Now this was fine. What was so exciting about making love with her was that she would have climaxes just by my cock being in her. All I had to do was enter her and she would have a climax and faint. Now, all right, maybe she was faking it, but at least it showed that she liked me. The relationship reached its romantic culmination when we ran out of *The Misanthrope* set and I leapt up naked, broke up the only remaining furniture in the room, threw it in the fireplace, and we made love in front of the burning chairs.

On Sundays Adriana would come over to my room to study. I'd get a fire going and she'd stretch out naked to read her botany book. After reading for a while, she'd fall asleep on her belly and I'd just stand there looking down at her exquisite naked ass and back. I could never get enough. This longing to devour her led to atomic bomb fantasies, which most likely grew out of a lot of my reading at the time. I had this fantasy that Adriana and I would commit atomic hari-kari together. I would have an atom bomb under my bed and just as we were about to come together, I would trigger it and the whole city of Boston would come and go with us.

With Adriana I had the sense that I was finally in love because I was jealous, really jealous, for the first time since Julie Brooks exchanged shirts with Billy Patterson. One day an old boyfriend of Adriana's came to Boston from New York and she was going over to pay him a short visit "just to catch up on old times," she said. I thought that meant "good times." While I was in the bathroom I looked up at the shelf over the toilet and noticed Adriana's diaphragm case, and thought, the sweet little thing, she's true to me. She actually left her diaphragm behind. But I had this little residue of doubt and I opened the case just to check. And the diaphragm was gone.

When Adriana returned that night we had a big fight. I went into a jealous rage. And she said, "Oh, babe. Don't you trust me? Do you really think I could make love to anyone else but you?" And I said, "Well, what the hell happened to your diaphragm then? Hey? What happened? You tell me!" She told me that it had sprung a leak, a little hole, and she had taken it into the diaphragm shop for repairs.

Soon after that I graduated from college, and I thought that graduation would mean the end of Adriana. But it didn't work that way, I missed her a lot. I was surprised at how much I missed her and I tracked her down at Block Island. I called her up from the mainland and said I was coming out. And she said, "Oh, I wouldn't do that." So I said, "What do you mean? I'll kill him! Kill him!" I couldn't believe I was talking like that. I was glad I was on the mainland. She said, "No, I don't think you should come out. I have a bad case of poison ivy." "I don't care about poison ivy," I said, and I went out anyway and she *did* have poison ivy, on her right thigh. We went to bed and made love and then in the morning she got out of bed while I was still asleep. I saw her disappearing through the sand dunes and I knew she was on her way to see him. I couldn't take it. I started crying and wandering up and down the beaches of Block Island, weeping, every so often looking over my shoulder at another woman on the beach.

I decided that this time I was going to become an asexual theater artist, and I went away to the Champlain Shakespeare Festival in Burlington, Vermont, with the anticipation of great roles. I had a roommate there that I didn't like. He was one of those actors who would recite Robert Frost poems by heart—"Two roads diverged in a yellow wood," and on and on and on. Both of us had our eyes on the same woman, a long, tall, dark woman who lived above us. But I was sticking to my vows. I was going to take my time even if it took all summer. I'd wait for her to come to me. My roommate didn't waste any time at all. The first night we were there I went off to a rehearsal. When I got back, I heard laughter coming from her second-storey balcony. I heard this Henry VIII laughter,

"Hah, hah hah hah hah." And I thought, my God, there ought to be a law, you know they just met! I was disgusted. And then I saw a naked leg rise up over the railing of the balcony just as her underwear came floating down and landed on my head. It was like a movie or a play. I took the underwear off my head, went inside and laid it on the guest bed next to mine, and went to sleep. I don't know how I slept.

The next morning when I got up, I took the panties upstairs to return them. I knocked on her door and she didn't answer. But the door was unlocked—it was Burlington, Vermont,—and I went in and left them on her bureau with a note. And shortly after that I was drafted.

[1986]

WHEN MAN ENTERS WOMAN

Anne Sexton

When man
enters woman,
like the surf biting the shore,
again and again,
and the woman opens her mouth in pleasure
and her teeth gleam
like the alphabet,
Logos appears milking a star,
and the man
inside of woman
ties a knot
so that they will
never again be separate
and the woman
climbs into a flower
and swallows its stem
and Logos appears
and unleashes their rivers.

This man,
this woman
with their double hunger,
have tried to reach through
the curtain of God
and briefly they have,
though God
in His perversity
unties the knot.

[1973]

WOMEN

Charles Bukowski

It was 3 or 4 days before I had to fly to Houston to give a reading. I went to the track, drank at the track, and afterwards I went to a bar on Hollywood Boulevard. I went home at 9 or 10 P.M. As I moved through the bedroom towards the bathroom I tripped over the telephone cord. I fell against the corner of the bed frame—an edge of steel like a knife blade. When I got up I found I had a deep gash just above the ankle. The blood ran into the rug and I left a bloody trail as I went to the bathroom. The blood ran over the tiles and I left red footprints as I walked about.

There was a knock on the door and I let Bobby in. "Jesus Christ, man, what happened?"

"It's DEATH," I said. "I'm bleeding to death. . . ."

"Man," he said, "you better do something about that leg."

Valerie knocked. I let her in too. She screamed. I poured Bobby and Valerie and myself drinks. The phone rang. It was Lydia.

"Lydia, baby, I'm bleeding to death!"

"Is this one of your dramatic trips again?"

"No, I'm bleeding to death. Ask Valerie."

Valerie took the phone. "It's true, his ankle is cut open. There's blood everywhere and he won't do anything about it. You better come over. . . ."

When Lydia arrived I was sitting on the couch. "Look, Lydia: DEATH!" Tiny veins were hanging out of the wound like strings of spaghetti. I yanked at some of them.

I took my cigarette and tapped ashes into the wound. "I'm a MAN! Hell, I'm a MAN!"

Lydia went and got some hydrogen peroxide and poured it into the wound. It was nice. White foam gushed out of the wound. It sizzled and bubbled. Lydia poured some more in.

"You better go to a hospital," Bobby said.

"I don't need a fucking hospital," I said. "It will cure itself. . . ."

The next morning the wound looked horrible. It was still open and seemed to be forming a nice crust. I went to the drugstore for some more hydrogen peroxide, some bandages, and some epsom salts. I filled the tub full of hot water and epsom salts and got in. I began thinking about myself with only one leg. There were advantages:

HENRY CHINASKI IS, WITHOUT A DOUBT, THE GREATEST ONE-LEGGED POET IN THE WORLD

Bobby came by that afternoon. "You know what it costs to get a leg amputated?"

"$12,000."

After Bobby left I phoned my doctor.

I went to Houston with a heavily bandaged leg. I was taking antibiotic pills in an attempt to cure the infection. My doctor mentioned that any drinking would nullify the good the antibiotic pills had.

At the reading, which was at the modern art museum, I went on sober. After I read a few poems somebody in the audience asked, "How come you're not drunk?"

"Henry Chinaski couldn't make it," I said. "I'm his brother Efram."

I read another poem and then confessed about the antibiotics. I also told them it was against museum rules to drink on the premises. Somebody from the audience came up with a beer. I drank it and read some more. Somebody else came up with another beer. Then the beers began to flow. The poems got better.

There was a party and a dinner afterwards at a cafe. Almost directly across the table from me was absolutely the most beautiful girl I had ever seen. She looked like a young Katherine Hepburn. She was about 22, and she just radiated beauty. I kept making wisecracks, calling her Katherine Hepburn. She seemed to like it. I didn't expect anything to come of it. She was with a girlfriend. When it came time to leave I said to the museum director, a woman named Nana, at whose house I was staying, "I'm going to miss her. She was too good to believe."

"She's coming home with us."

"I don't believe it."

. . . but later there she was, at Nana's place, in the bedroom with me. She had on a sheer nightgown, and she sat on the edge of the bed combing her very long hair and smiling at me. "What's your name?" I asked.

"Laura," she said.

"Well, look, Laura, I'm going to call you Katherine."

"All right," she said.

Her hair was reddish-brown and so very long. She was small but well proportioned. Her face was the most beautiful thing about her.

"Can I pour you a drink?" I asked.

"Oh no, I don't drink. I don't like it."

Actually, she frightened me. I couldn't understand what she was doing there with me. She didn't appear to be a groupie. I went to the bathroom, came back and turned out the light. I could feel her getting into bed next to me. I took her in my arms and we began kissing. I couldn't believe my luck. What right had I? How could a few books of poems call this forth? There was no way to understand it. I certainly was not about to reject it. I became very aroused. Suddenly she went down and took my cock in her mouth. I watched the slow movement of her head and body in the moonlight. She wasn't as good at it as some, but it was the very fact of *her* doing it that was amazing. Just as I was about to come I reached down and buried my hand in that mass of beautiful hair, pulling at it in the moonlight as I came in Katherine's mouth.

Lydia met me at the airport. She was horny as usual.

"Jesus Christ," she said. "I'm *hot!* I play with myself but it doesn't do any good."

We were driving back to my place.

"Lydia, my leg is still in terrible shape. I just don't know if I can handle it with this leg."

"What?"

"It's true. I don't think I can fuck with my leg the way it is."

"What the hell good are you then?"

"Well, I can fry eggs and do magic tricks."

"Don't be funny. I'm asking you, what the hell good are you?"

"The leg will heal. If it doesn't they'll cut it off. Be patient."

"If you hadn't been drunk you wouldn't have fallen and cut your leg. It's *always* the bottle!"

"It's not always the bottle, Lydia. We fuck about 4 times a week. For my age that's pretty good."

"Sometimes I think you don't even enjoy it."

"Lydia, sex isn't *everything!* You are obsessed. For Christ's sake, give it a rest."

"A rest until your leg heals? How am I going to make it meanwhile?"

"I'll play Scrabble with you."

Lydia screamed. The car began to swerve all over the street. "YOU SON-OF-A-BITCH! I'LL KILL YOU!"

She crossed the double yellow line at high speed, directly into oncoming traffic. Horns sounded and cars scattered. We drove on against the flow of traffic, cars approaching us peeling off to the left and right. Then just as abruptly Lydia swerved back across the double line into the lane we had just vacated.

Where are the police? I thought. Why is it that when Lydia does something the police become nonexistent?

"All right," she said. "I'm taking you home and that's it. I've had it. I'm going to sell my house and move to Phoenix. Glendoline lives in Phoenix now. My sisters warned me about living with an old fuck like you."

We drove the remainder of the way without talking. When we reached my place I took out my suitcase, looked at Lydia, said, "Goodbye." She was crying without making a sound, her whole face was wet. Suddenly she drove off toward Western Avenue. I walked into the court. Back from another reading. . . .

I checked the mail and then phoned Katherine who lived in Austin, Texas. She seemed truly glad to hear from me, and it was good to hear that Texas accent, that high laughter. I told her that I wanted her to come visit me, that I'd pay air fare both ways. We'd go to the racetrack, we'd go to Malibu, we'd . . . whatever she wanted. "But, Hank, don't you have a girlfriend?"

"No, none. I'm a recluse."

"But you're always writing about women in your poems."

"That's past. This is present."

"But what about Lydia?"

"Lydia?"

"Yes, you told me all about her."

"What did I tell you?"

"You told me how she beat up two other women. Would you let her beat me up? I'm not very big, you know."

"It can't happen. She's moved to Phoenix. I tell you, Katherine, you are *the* exceptional woman I've been looking for. Please, trust me."

"I'll have to make arrangements. I have to get somebody to take care of my cat."

"All right. But I want you to know that everything is clear here."

"But, Hank, don't forget what you told me about your women."

"Told you what?"

"You said, 'They always come back.'"

"That's just macho talk."

"I'll come," she said. "As soon as I get things straight here I'll make a reservation and let you know the details."

When I was in Texas Katherine had told me about her life. I was only the third man she had slept with. There had been her husband, an alcoholic track star, and me. Her ex-husband, Arnold, was into show business and the arts in some way. Exactly how it worked I didn't know. He was continually signing contracts with rock stars, painters and so forth. The business was $60,000 in debt, but flourishing. One of those situations where the further you were in debt the better off you were.

I don't know what happened to the track star. He just ran off, I guess. And then Arnold got on coke. The coke changed him overnight. Katherine said she didn't know him anymore. It was terrifying. Ambulance trips to hospitals. And then he'd be back at the office the next morning as if nothing had happened. Then Joanna Dover entered the picture. A tall, stately semi-millionairess. Educated and crazy. She and Arnold began to do business together. Joanna Dover dealt in the arts like some people deal in corn futures. She discovered unknown artists on the way up, bought their work cheap, and sold high after they became recognized. She had that kind of eye. And a magnificent 6-foot body. She began to see a lot of Arnold. One evening Joanna came to pick up Arnold dressed in an expensive tight-fitting gown. Then Katherine knew that Joanna really meant business. So, after that, she went along whenever Arnold and Joanna would go out. They were a trio. Arnold had a *very* low sex drive, so Katherine wasn't worried about that. She was worried about the business. Then Joanna dropped out of the picture, and Arnold got more and more into coke. More and more ambulance trips. Katherine finally divorced him. She still saw Arnold, however. She took coffee to the office at 10:30 every morning for the staff and Arnold put her on the payroll. Which enabled her to keep the house. She and Arnold had dinner there now and then, but no sex. Still, he needed her, she felt protective towards him. Katherine also believed in health foods and the only meat she ate was chicken and fish. She was a beautiful woman.

Within a day or two, about 1 P.M. in the afternoon there was a knock at my door. It was a painter, Monty Riff, or so he informed me. He also told me that I used to get drunk with him when I lived on DeLongpre Avenue.

"I don't remember you," I said.

"Dee Dee used to bring me over."

"Oh yeah? Well, come on in." Monty had a 6-pack with him and a tall stately woman.

"This is Joanna Dover," he introduced me to her.

"I missed your reading in Houston," she said.

"Laura Stanley told me all about you," I said.

"You know her?"

"Yes. But I've renamed her Katherine, after Katherine Hepburn."

"You really *know* her?"

"Fairly well."

"How well?"

"She's flying out to visit me in a day or two."

"Really?"

"Yes."

We finished the 6-pack and I left to go get some more. When I got back Monty was gone. Joanna told me that he had an appointment. We got to talking about painting and I brought out some of mine. She looked at them and decided that she'd like to buy two of them. "How much?" she asked.

"Well, $40 for the small one and $60 for the large one."

Joanna wrote me out a check for $100. Then she said, "I want you to live with me."

"What? This is pretty sudden."

"It would pay off. I have some money. Just don't ask me how much. I've been thinking of some reasons why we should live together. Do you want to hear them?"

"No."

"One thing, if we lived together I'd take you to Paris."

"I hate to travel."

"I'd show you a Paris you'd really like."

"Let me think it over."

I leaned over and gave her a kiss. Then I kissed her again, this time a little longer.

"Shit," I said, "let's go to bed."

"All right," said Joanna Dover.

We undressed and climbed in. She was 6 feet tall. I'd always had small women. It was strange—every place I reached there seemed to be more woman. We warmed up. I gave her 3 or 4 minutes of oral sex, then mounted. She was good, she was really good. We cleaned up, got dressed and then she took me to dinner in Malibu. She told me she lived in Galveston, Texas. She gave me her phone number, the address and told me to come and see her. I told her that I would. She told me that she was serious about Paris and the rest. It had been a good fuck and the dinner was excellent too.

The next day Katherine phoned me. She said she had the tickets and would be landing at L.A. International Friday at 2:30 P.M.

"Katherine," I said, "there's something I've got to tell you."

"Hank, don't you want to see me?"

"I want to see you more than anybody I know."

"Then what is it?"

"Well, you know Joanna Dover . . ."

"Joanna Dover?"

"The one . . . you know . . . your husband . . ."

"What about her, Hank?"

"Well, she came to see me."

"You mean she came to your place?"

"Yes."

"What happened?"

"We talked. She bought two of my paintings."

"Anything else happen?"

"Yeah."

Katherine was quiet. Then she said, "Hank, I don't know if I want to see you now."

"I understand. Look, why don't you think it over and call me back? I'm sorry, Katherine. I'm sorry it happened. That's all I can say."

She hung up. She won't phone back, I thought. The best woman I ever met and I blew it. I deserve defeat, I deserve to die alone in a madhouse.

I sat by the telephone. I read the newspaper, the sports section, the financial section, the funny papers. The phone rang. It was Katherine. "FUCK Joanna Dover!" she laughed. I'd never heard Katherine swear like that before.

"Then you're coming?"

"Yes. Do you have the arrival time?"

"I have it all. I'll be there."

We said goodbye. Katherine was coming, she was coming for at least a week with that face, that body, that hair, those eyes, that laugh. . . .

I came out of the bar and checked the message board. The plane was on time. Katherine was in the air and moving towards me. I sat down and waited. Across from me was a well-groomed woman reading a paperback. Her dress was up around her thighs, showing all that flank, that leg wrapped in nylon. Why did she insist on doing that? I had a newspaper, and I looked over the top, up her dress. She had great thighs. Who was getting those thighs? I felt foolish staring up her dress, but I couldn't help myself. She was built. Once she had been a little girl, someday she would be dead, but now she was showing me her upper legs. The goddamned strumpet, I'd give her a hundred strokes, I'd give her 7-and-one-half inches of throbbing purple! She crossed her legs and her dress inched higher.

She looked up from her paperback. Her eyes looked into mine as I watched over the top of the newspaper. Her expression was indifferent. She reached into her purse and took out a stick of gum, took the wrapper off and put the gum in her mouth. Green gum. She chewed on the green gum and I watched her mouth. She didn't pull her skirt down. She knew that I was looking. There was nothing I could do. I opened my wallet and took out 2 fifty dollar bills. She looked up, saw the bills, looked back down. Then a fat man plopped down next to me. His face was very red and he had a massive nose. He was dressed in a jumpsuit, a light brown jumpsuit. He farted. The lady pulled her dress down and I put the bills back in my wallet. My cock softened and I got up and went to the drinking fountain.

Out in the landing area Katherine's plane was taxiing towards the ramp. I stood and waited. Katherine, I adore you.

Katherine walked off the ramp, perfect, with red-brown hair, slim body, a blue dress clinging as she walked, white shoes, slim, neat ankles, youth. She wore a white hat with a wide brim, the brim turned down just right. Her eyes looked out from under the brim, large and brown and laughing. She had class. She'd never show her ass in an airport waiting area.

And there I was, 225 pounds, perpetually lost and confused, short legs, ape-like upper body, all chest, no neck, head too large, blurred eyes, hair uncombed, 6 feet of geek, waiting for her.

Katherine moved towards me. That long clean red-brown hair. Texas women were so relaxed, so natural. I gave her a kiss and asked about her baggage. I suggested we stop at the bar. The waitresses had on short red dresses that showed their ruffled white panties. The necklines of their dresses were cut low to show their breasts. They earned their salaries, they earned their tips, every cent.

They lived in the suburbs and they hated men. They lived with their mothers and brothers and were in love with their psychiatrists.

We finished our drinks and went to get Katherine's baggage. A number of men tried to catch her eye, but she walked close by my side, holding my arm. Few beautiful women were willing to indicate in public that they belonged to someone. I had known enough women to realize this. I accepted them for what they were, and love came hard and very seldom. When it did it was usually for the wrong reasons. One simply became tired of holding love back and let it go because it *needed* some place to go. Then usually, there was trouble.

At my place Katherine opened her suitcase and took out a pair of rubber gloves. She laughed.

"What is this?" I asked.

"Darlene—my best friend—she saw me packing and she said, 'What the hell are you *doing?*' And I said, 'I've never seen Hank's place, but I *know* that before I can cook in it and live in it and sleep in it I've got to clean it up!'"

Then Katherine gave off that happy Texas laugh. She went into the bathroom and put on a pair of bluejeans and an orange blouse, came out barefooted and went into the kitchen with her rubber gloves.

I went into the bathroom and changed clothes too. I decided that if Lydia came by I'd never let her touch Katherine. Lydia? Where was she? What was she doing?

I sent up a little prayer to the gods who watched over me: please keep Lydia away. Let her suck on the horns of cowboys and dance until 3 A.M.—but please keep her away. . . .

When I came out Katherine was on her knees scrubbing at two years' worth of grease on my kitchen floor.

"Katherine," I said, "let's go out of town. Let's go have dinner. This is no way to begin."

"All right, Hank, but I've got to finish this floor first. Then we'll go."

I sat and waited. Then she came out and I was sitting in a chair, waiting. She bent over and kissed me, laughing, "You *are* a dirty old man!" Then she walked into the bedroom. I was in love again, I was in trouble. . . .

After dinner we came back and we talked. She was a health food addict and didn't eat meat except for chicken and fish. It certainly worked for her.

"Hank," she said, "tomorrow I'm going to clean your bathroom."

"All right," I said over my drink.

"And I must do my exercise every day. Will that bother you?"

"No, no."

"Will you be able to write while I'm fussing around here?"

"No problem."

"I can go for walks."

"No, not alone, not in this neighborhood."

"I don't want to interfere with your writing."

"There's no way I can stop writing, it's a form of insanity."

Katherine came over and sat by me on the couch. She seemed more a girl than a woman. I put down my drink and kissed her, a long, slow kiss. Her lips were cool and soft. I was very conscious of her long red-brown hair. I pulled away and had another drink. She confused me. I was used to vile drunken wenches.

We talked for another hour. "Let's go to sleep," I told her, "I'm tired."

"Fine. I'll get ready first," she said.

I sat drinking. I needed more to drink. She simply was too much.

"Hank," she said, "I'm in bed."

"All right."

I went into the bathroom and undressed, brushed my teeth, washed my face and hands. She came all the way from Texas, I thought, she came on a plane just to see me and now she's in my bed, waiting.

I didn't have any pyjamas. I walked towards the bed. She was in a nightie. "Hank," she said, "we have about 6 days when it's safe, then we'll have to think of something else."

I got into bed with her. The little girl-woman was ready. I pulled her towards me. Luck was mine again, the gods were smiling. The kisses became more intense. I placed her hand on my cock and then pulled up her nightie. I began to play with her cunt. Katherine with a cunt? The clit came out and I touched it gently, again and again. Finally, I mounted. My cock entered halfway. It was very tight. I moved it back and forth, then pushed. The remainder of my cock slid in. It was glorious. She gripped me. I moved and her grip held. I tried to control myself. I stopped stroking and waited to cool off. I kissed her, working her lips apart, sucking at the upper lip. I saw her hair spread wide across the pillow. Then I gave up trying to please her and simply fucked her, ripping viciously. It was like murder. I didn't care; my cock had gone crazy. All that hair, her young and beautiful face. It was like raping the Virgin Mary. I came. I came inside of her, agonizing, feeling my sperm enter her body, she was helpless, and I shot my come deep into her ultimate core—body and soul—again and again. . . .

Later on, we slept. Or Katherine slept. I held her from the back. For the first time I thought of marriage. I knew that there certainly were flaws in her that had not surfaced. The beginning of a relationship was always the easiest. After that the unveiling began, never to stop. Still, I thought of marriage. I thought of a house, a dog and a cat, of shopping in supermarkets. Henry Chinaski was losing his balls. And didn't care.

At last I slept. When I awakened in the morning Katherine was sitting on the edge of the bed brushing those yards of red-brown hair. Her large dark eyes looked at me as I awakened. "Hello, Katherine," I said, "will you marry me?"

"Please don't," she said, "I don't like it."

"I mean it."

"Oh, *shit,* Hank!"

"What?"

"I said, 'shit,' and if you talk that way I'm taking the first plane out."

"All right."

"Hank?"

"Yes?"

I looked at Katherine. She kept brushing her long hair. Her large brown eyes looked at me, and she was smiling. She said, "It's just *sex,* Hank, it's *just sex!*" Then she laughed. It wasn't a sardonic laugh, it was really joyful. She brushed her hair and I put my arm around her waist and rested my head against her leg. I wasn't quite sure of anything.

I took women either to the boxing matches or to the racetrack. That Thursday night I took Katherine to the boxing matches at the Olympic auditorium. She had never been to a live fight. We got there before the first bout and sat at ringside. I drank beer and smoked and waited.

"It's strange," I told her, "that people will sit here and

wait for two men to climb up there into that ring and try to punch each other out."

"It does seem awful."

"This place was built a long time ago," I told her as she looked around the ancient arena. "There are only two restrooms, one for men, the other for women, and they are small. So try to go before or after intermission."

"All right."

The Olympic was attended mostly by Latinos and lower class working whites, with a few movie stars and celebrities. There were many good Mexican fighters and they fought with their hearts. The only bad fights were when whites or blacks fought, especially the heavyweights.

Being there with Katherine felt strange. Human relationships were strange. I mean, you were with one person a while, eating and sleeping and living with them, loving them, talking to them, going places together, and then it stopped. Then there was a short period when you weren't with anybody, then another woman arrived, and you ate with her and fucked her, and it all seemed so normal, as if you had been waiting just for her and she had been waiting for you. I never felt right being alone; sometimes it felt good but it never felt right.

The first fight was a good one, lots of blood and courage. There was something to be learned about writing from watching boxing matches or going to the racetrack. The message wasn't clear but it helped me. That was the important part: the message wasn't clear. It was wordless, like a house burning, or an earthquake or a flood, or a woman getting out of a car, showing her legs. I didn't know what other writers needed; I didn't care, I couldn't read them anyway. I was locked into my own habits, my own prejudices. It wasn't bad being dumb *if* the ignorance was all your own. I knew that some day I would write about Katherine and that it would be hard. It was easy to write about whores, but to write about a good woman was much more difficult.

The second fight was good, too. The crowd screamed and roared and swilled beer. They had temporarily escaped the factories, the warehouses, the slaughterhouses, the car washes—they'd be back in captivity the next day but *now* they were out—they were wild with freedom. They weren't thinking about the slavery of poverty. Or the slavery of welfare and food stamps. The rest of us would be all right until the poor learned how to make atom bombs in their basements.

All the fights were good. I got up and went to the restroom. When I got back Katherine was very still. She looked more like she should be attending a ballet or a concert. She looked so delicate and yet she was such a marvelous fuck.

I kept drinking and Katherine would grab one of my hands when a fight became exceptionally brutal. The crowd loved knockouts. They screamed when one of the fighters was on the way out. *They* were landing those punches. Maybe they were punching out their bosses or their wives. Who knew? Who cared? More beer.

I suggested to Katherine that we leave before the final bout. I'd had enough.

"All right," she said.

We walked up the narrow aisle, the air blue with smoke. There was no whistling, no obscene gestures. My scarred and battered face was sometimes an asset.

We walked back to the small parking lot under the freeway. The '67 blue Volks was not there. The '67 model was the last good Volks—and the young men knew it.

"Hepburn, they stole our fucking car."

"Oh Hank, surely not!"

"It's gone. It was sitting there." I pointed. "Now it's gone."

"Hank, what will we do?"

"We'll take a taxi. I really feel bad."

"Why do people do that?"

"They have to. It's their way out."

We went into a coffee shop and I phoned for a cab. We ordered coffee and doughnuts. While we had been watching the fights they had pulled the coathanger and hotwire trick. I had a saying, "Take my woman, but leave my car alone." I would never kill a man who took my woman; I might kill a man who took my car.

The cab came. At my place, luckily, there was beer and some vodka. I had given up all hope of staying sober enough to make love. Katherine knew it. I paced up and down talking about my '67 blue Volks. The last good model. I couldn't even call the police. I was too drunk. I'd have to wait until morning, until noon.

"Hepburn," I told her, "it's not *your* fault, *you* didn't steal it!"

"I wish I had, you'd have it now."

I thought of 2 or 3 young kids racing my blue baby down along the Coast Highway, smoking dope, laughing, opening it up. Then I thought of all the junkyards along Santa Fe Avenue. Mountains of bumpers, windshields, doorhandles, wiper motors, engine parts, tires, wheels, hoods, jacks, bucket seats, front wheel bearings, brake shoes, radios, pistons, valves, carburetors, cam shafts, transmissions, axles—my car soon would be just a pile of accessories.

That night I slept up against Katherine, but my heart was sad and cold.

Luckily I had auto insurance that paid for a rental car. I drove Katherine to the racetrack in it. We sat in the sundeck at Hollywood Park near the stretch turn. Katherine said she didn't want to bet but I took her inside and showed her the toteboard and the betting windows.

I put 5 win on a 7 to 2 shot with early lick, my favorite kind of horse. I always figured if you're going to lose you might as well lose in front; you had the race won until somebody beat you. The horse went wire to wire, pulling away at the end. It paid $9.40 and I was $17.50 ahead.

The next race she remained in her seat while I went to make my bet. When I came back she pointed to a man two rows below us. "See that man there?"

"Yes."

"He told me he won $2,000 yesterday and that he's $25,000 ahead for the meet."

"Don't you want to bet? Maybe we all can win."

"Oh no, I don't know anything about it."

"It's simple: you give them a dollar and they give you 84 cents back. It's called the 'take.' The state and the track split it about even. They don't care *who* wins the race, their take is out of the total mutual pool."

In the second race my horse, the 8 to 5 favorite, ran second. A longshot had nosed me at the wire. It paid $45.80.

The man two rows down turned and looked at Katherine. "I had it," he told her, "I had ten on the nose."

"Oooh," she told him, smiling, "that's good."

I turned to the third race, an affair for 2-year-old maiden colts and geldings. At 5 minutes to post I checked the tote and went to bet. As I walked away I saw the man two rows down turn and begin talking to Katherine. There were at least a dozen of them at the track every day, who told attractive women what big winners they were, hoping that somehow they would end up in bed with them. Maybe they didn't even think that far; maybe they only hoped vaguely for something without being quite sure what it was. They were addled and dizzied, taking the 10-count. Who could hate them? Big winners, but if you watched them bet, they were usually at the 2 dollar window, their shoes down at the heels and their clothing dirty. The lowest of the breed.

I took the even money shot and he won by 6 and paid $4.00. Not much, but I had him ten win. The man turned around and looked at Katherine. "I had it," he told her. "$100 to win."

Katherine didn't answer. She was beginning to understand. Winners didn't shoot off their mouths. They were afraid of getting murdered in the parking lot.

After the fourth race, a $22.80 winner, he turned again and told Katherine, "I had that one, ten across."

She turned away. "His face is yellow, Hank. Did you see his eyes? He's sick."

"He's sick on the dream. We're all sick on the dream, that's why we're out here."

"Hank, let's go."

"All right."

That night she drank half a bottle of red wine, good red wine, and she was sad and quiet. I knew she was connecting me with the racetrack people and the boxing crowd, and it was true, I was with them, I was one of them. Katherine knew that there was something about me that was not wholesome in the sense of wholesome is as wholesome does. I was drawn to all the wrong things: I liked to drink, I was lazy, I didn't have a god, politics, ideas, ideals. I was settled into nothingness; a kind of non-being, and I accepted it. It didn't make for an interesting person. I didn't want to be interesting, it was too hard. What I really wanted was only a soft, hazy space to live in, and to be left alone. On the other hand, when I got drunk

I screamed, went crazy, got all out of hand. One kind of behavior didn't fit the other. I didn't care.

The fucking was very good that night, but it was the night I lost her. There was nothing I could do about it. I rolled off and wiped myself on the sheet as she went into the bathroom. Overhead a police helicopter circled over Hollywood.

The next night Bobby and Valerie came over. They had recently moved into my apartment building and now lived across the court. Bobby had on his tight knit shirt. Everything always fitted Bobby perfectly, his pants were snug and just the right length, he wore the right shoes and his hair was styled. Valerie also dressed mod but not quite as consciously. People called them the "Barbie Dolls." Valerie was all right when you got her alone, she was intelligent and very energetic and damned honest. Bobby, too, was more human when he and I were alone, but when a new woman was around he became very dull and obvious. He would direct all his attention and conversation to the woman, as if his very presence was an interesting and marvelous thing, but his conversation became predictable and dull. I wondered how Katherine would handle him.

They sat down. I was in a chair near the window and Valerie sat between Bobby and Katherine on the couch. Bobby began. He bent forward and ignoring Valerie directed his attention to Katherine.

"Do you like Los Angeles?" he asked.

"It's all right," answered Katherine.

"Are you going to stay here much longer?"

"A while longer."

"You're from Texas?"

"Yes."

"Are your parents from Texas?"

"Yes."

"Anything good on t.v. out there?"

"It's about the same."

"I've got an uncle in Texas."

"Oh."

"Yes, he lives in Dallas."

Katherine didn't answer. Then she said, "Excuse me, I'm going to make a sandwich. Does anybody want anything?"

We said we didn't. Katherine got up and went into the kitchen. Bobby got up and followed her. You couldn't quite hear his words, but you could tell that he was asking more questions. Valerie stared at the floor. Katherine and Bobby were in the kitchen a long time. Suddenly Valerie raised her head and began talking to me. She spoke very rapidly and nervously.

"Valerie," I stopped her, "we needn't talk, we don't have to talk."

She put her head down again.

Then I said, "Hey, you guys have been in there a long time. Are you waxing the floor?"

Bobby laughed and began tapping his foot in rhythm on the floor.

Finally Katherine came out followed by Bobby. She walked over to me and showed me her sandwich: peanut butter on cracked wheat with sliced bananas and sesame seeds.

"It looks good," I told her.

She sat down and began eating her sandwich. It became quiet. It remained quiet. Then Bobby said, "Well, I think we'd better go. . . ."

They left. After the door closed Katherine looked at me and said, "Don't think anything, Hank. He was just trying to impress me."

"He's done that with every woman I've known since I've known him."

The phone rang. It was Bobby. "Hey, man, what have you done to my wife?"

"What's the matter?"

"She just *sits* here, she's completely depressed, she won't talk!"

"I haven't done anything to your wife."

"I don't understand it!"

"Goodnight, Bobby."

I hung up.

"It was Bobby," I told Katherine. "His wife is depressed."

"Really?"

"It seems so."

"Are you sure you don't want a sandwich?"

"Can you make me one just like yours?"

"Oh, yes."

"I'll take it."

Katherine stayed 4 or 5 more days. We had reached the time of the month when it was risky for Katherine to fuck. I couldn't stand rubbers. Katherine got some contraceptive foam. Meanwhile, the police had recovered my Volks. We went down to where it was impounded. It was intact and in good shape except for a dead battery. I had it hauled to a Hollywood garage where they put it in order. After a last goodbye in bed I drove Katherine to the airport in the blue Volks, TRV 469.

It wasn't a happy day for me. We sat not saying much. Then they called her flight and we kissed.

"Hey, they all saw this young girl kissing this old man."

"I don't give a damn. . . ."

Katherine kissed me again.

"You're going to miss your flight," I said.

"Come see me, Hank. I have a nice house. I live alone. Come see me."

"I will."

"Write!"

"I will. . . ."

Katherine walked into the boarding tunnel and was gone.

I walked back to the parking lot, got in the Volks, thinking, I've still got this. What the hell, I haven't lost everything.

It started.

[1978]

PREFACE TO A BOOK OF CIGARETTE PAPERS

Don Marquis

One of our youthful ambitions was to be able to sit astride a horse, governing his action with one hand while with the other we nonchalantly rolled a cigarette. We have never known but two people who could do it. One of them was employed by a show, and we always suspected that there was an understanding, a gentlemen's agreement, between the horse and him; perhaps he bribed the animal outright. The other was a genuine cowboy who had gone to the real West from the little middle western country town where we lived more than thirty years ago and who liked to come back "East" for a few weeks every two or three years and exhibit tricks of the sort before an admiring crowd of former friends and neighbors. His name was Buck Something-or-Other.

No doubt among his fellow range riders a few hundred miles to the west Buck was commonplace enough, but to our tame Illinois village, where nothing ever happened, Buck was a figure of romance. He was a being from another world, a link between the paper covered novels which we read and real life. Perhaps he knew it and enjoyed being just that; he was a picturesque and facile liar; likely he read the paper covered novels too and was consciously striving to suggest their heroes—a thing he could get away with much more readily in Illinois than in the West, we suppose.

At any rate it was from Buck that we gained our original impression that there was something rather elegant and dashing and picturesque and knowing about the cigarette. We never did learn to roll them with one hand, either on a horse or off of one; to this day it is all we can do to roll one that will hang together, seated securely in an armchair and using all our fingers and thumbs, and we have more thumbs than any one else we know when it comes to a business of that sort.

The mind of youth is "wax to receive and marble to retain," as a friend of ours once quoted while observing a family of six children, all below the age of ten, being dragged through the horror chamber of the Eden Musée. And there still dwells within us the feeling that the rolled cigarette belongs of right to such interesting creatures as adventurers and revolutionists and poets.

We had been a worshiper of Stevenson for some time before we learned that he was addicted to them, and when we learned it the circumstance naturally confirmed our feeling. Personally we do not enjoy smoking them; we do not get any physical satisfaction out of them; this is due, no doubt, to the fact that we learned to smoke a corncob pipe crammed with the very rankest and blackest tobacco at an early age, and no cigarette means anything to us unless we chew it as a goat or a deer chews them.

But it is the grosser and more material side of our nature which finds the cigarette too feeble and pallid; all that is romantic and literary and spiritual in us holds by the cigarette. When we die and are purged of all the heavy flesh that holds us down, our soul, we hope, will roll and smoke cigarettes along with Buck the romantic and lying cowboy and Ariel and Stevenson and Benvenuto Cellini and Jack Hamlin. We have never been the person on earth we should like to be; circumstances have always tied us to the staid and commonplace and respectable; but when we become an angel we hope to be right devilish at times.

And that is an idea that some one should work out—Hell as a place of reward for Puritans. But it is possible that that elderly Mephistopheles, with the smack of a canting Calvinistic archangel about him, Bernard Shaw, has already done so somewhere.

Where the idea that the cigarette is more injurious than tobacco taken in any other form originated we cannot imagine. It seems to us, looking back and looking round on all the smokers we have known and know, to be grotesquely untrue. But we believed it firmly in our youth; it added a spice of deviltry to the idea of cigarette smoking which made it ten times more attractive. We dare say that scores of thousands, and perhaps millions, of American boys have taken to cigarette smoking simply because they thought it more reckless than smoking cigars or pipes. The moralists managed to invest it for them with a mysterious tradition of depravity; and so, quite naturally, having arrived at a certain age, they took to it enthusiastically. It has probably been a good thing for them; it has kept them away from too much pipe and cigar smoking. If we had been encouraged by some farsighted elder relation to take to cigarettes at the age of ten we should not be the physically ruinous thing, the anemic, pipe-shattered wreck, that we are today. But, as we have said, the mild things give us no sensation unless we eat them; and now it is too late for us to reform and take them up.

[1919]

THE VOCABULARY OF THE DRINKING CHAMBER

H. L. Mencken

Bartenders, as a class, are probably the most adept practical psychologists on earth, but they have never given much attention to purely humanistic studies, as, for example, semantics. One result is that their professional argot is pretty meager; indeed, it might reasonably be described as infirm. At least ninety-five per cent of them, in speaking of the tools and *materia* of their craft, use the threadbare words of every day. A glass, to them, is simply a *glass,* a bung starter is a *bung starter,* a bouncer is a *bouncer,* rye whiskey is *rye,* a cocktail is a *cocktail,* gin is *gin,* and so on *ad finem.* There are, to be sure, occasional Winchells among them, but no such Winchell has ever concocted anything to raise the hackles of a linguistic pathologist. When they call a garrulous client an *auctioneer,* or a *souse* a *trance,* he barely flutters an eyelid, nor does he find much to lift him in *squirt gun* for a Seltzer siphon, *sham* for a glass with a false bottom, *stick* for the handle of a beer spigot, or *comb* for the instrument that slices off the supererogatory suds from a stoup of beer. Even *cop's bottle* for the worst whiskey in the house seems to him to be close to the obvious; what else, indeed, could it be called? College boys, in their opprobrious names for their books, their professors, and the females who prey upon them, have developed a great many niftier and hotter words, and railroad men, to cite only one group of workingmen, have invented so rich and bizarre a vocabulary that it transcends the poor jargon of the booze slingers as the spiral nebula in Andromeda transcends the flash of a match.

A good way to discover the paucity of bartenders' neologistic powers is to ask yourself what they call themselves. Have they ever invented a fancy name comparable to the *mortician* of the undertakers, the *realtor* of the real-estate jobbers, the *ecdysiast* of the strip teasers, or the *cosmetologist* of the beauté-shoppé gals? Alas, they have not, and it seems very unlikely that they ever will. Even so silly a term as *mixologist* was devised not by a practicing bartender but by some forgotten journalist writing in the *Knickerbocker Magazine* in 1856. He intended it sportively and it has remained on that level ever since, along with *colonel* for a whiskey drummer and *professor* for a kneader of pugilists. In 1901, the *Police Gazette,* then at the apex of its educational influence, attempted to revive and glorify *mixologist,* but the effort failed miserably, and *bar clerk* was soon substituted, and likewise failed. *Barman,* borrowed from the English, has been put forward from time to time, and there used to be an International *Barmen* Association in New York, but I can no longer find it in the Manhattan telephone book, and its former spot is now held by the International *Bartenders* School, on Forty-sixth Street, which has a Yale for its Harvard in the *Bartenders* School, Inc., on Forty-ninth Street. Both have excellent reputations in scholastic circles. All the existing unions in the profession, so far as I have been able to track them down, use plain *bartender* in their titles, and so do the various social clubs, choral societies, and leagues against prohibition and Communism. Some time ago, Oscar Haimo, of the Hotel Pierre, described himself as *maître de bar* in the advertising of his latest book, "Cocktails and Wine Digest," but I have yet to hear a second for it. Nor is there any visible support for *server,* which made its début in New

Jersey late in 1910 and seems to have died the death by January 1, 1911. Forgetting the vulgar *barkeeper* and *barkeep,* only *bartender* survives, a lowly word but a sound one. It arose from unknown sources during the Gothic Age of American boozing, *c.* 1855, and is of purely American genesis, though the English now toy with it. So is *barroom,* which was used by John Adams in 1807. And so is *bar* (the room, not the service counter), which was first heard of in 1788. The English *barmaid* has never caught on in this country; perhaps it suggests too strongly the poetic but smelly *milkmaid.* There are many females behind our more democratic bars, and I know one in Baltimore who is a first-rate artist, but if you called her a *barmaid,* she would crown you with the cop's bottle.

The failure of the bartenders to enrich the vocabulary of their art and mystery is matched by the reluctance of professional philologians to investigate the terms already existing. This reluctance, of course, may be due to the fact that booze studies are frowned upon on most college campuses, and hence bring no promotion to the ambitious pedagogue; also, there may be something in the fact that men learned in the tongues commonly carry their liquor badly, and sometimes have to be sent home from their annual powwows in charge of trained nurses. Whatever the truth about this, it remains a matter of record that they have done next to nothing to clear up the etymologies of boozology and that the origins of many of our salient drinking terms—for example, *cocktail, Mickey Finn,* and *highball*—are quite as dark as the origins of the things themselves. In this emergency, as might be expected, a great many amateurs have thrown themselves into the breach, and the result is a mass of surmise and speculation that gives the scientific student a lot of pain. I have in my archives perhaps forty or fifty such etymologies for *cocktail,* but can only report sadly that nearly all of them are no more than baloney. The most plausible that I have encountered was launched upon humanity by Stanley Clisby Arthur, author of "Famous New Orleans Drinks and How to Mix Them," a classical work. It is to the effect that the *cocktail* was invented, along about 1800, by Antoine Amédée Peychaud, a refugee from Santo Domingo who operated a New Orleans pharmacy in the Rue Royale. This Peychaud was a Freemason, and his brethren in the craft took to dropping in at his drugstore after their lodge meetings. A hospitable fellow, he regaled them with a toddy made of French brandy, sugar, water, and a bitters of a secret formula, brought from Santo Domingo. Apparently running short of toddy glasses, he served this mixture in double-ended eggcups, called, in French *"coquetiers."* The true pronunciation of the word was something on the order of *"ko-kayt-yay,"* but his American friends soon mangled it to *"cock-tay"* and then to *"cocktail."* The composition of the bitters he used remained secret, and they are known as Peychaud's to this day. His brandy came from the Sazerac du Forge et Fils distillery at Limoges, and its name survives in the Sazerac cocktail, though this powerful drug is now usually made of rye whiskey, with the addition of Peychaud's bitters, absinthe, lemon peel, and sugar.

As I have said, this etymology has more plausibility than most, and I'd like to believe it, if only to ease my mind, but some obvious question marks follow it. First, why didn't Arthur give his authorities? It is hard to believe that he remembered back to 1800 himself, and if there were intervening chroniclers, then why didn't he name them? And if he got his facts from original documents— say, in the old Cabildo—then why didn't he supply titles, dates, and pages? A greater difficulty lies in the fact that the searchers for the "Dictionary of American English" unearthed a plain mention of the *cocktail* in the Hudson (N.Y.) *Balance* for May 13, 1806, in which it was defined as "a stimulating liquor composed of spirits of any kind, sugar, water, and bitters." How did Peychaud's invention, if it *was* his invention, make its way from New Orleans to so remote a place as Hudson, New York, in so short a time, and how did it become generalized on the way? At the start of its journey it was a concoction of very precise composition—as much so as the Martini or Manhattan of today—but in a very few years it was popping up more than a thousand miles away, with an algebraic formula, $x + C_{12}H_{22}O_{11} + H_2O + y$, that can be developed, by substitution, into almost countless other formulas, all of them making authentic cocktails. Given *any* hard liquor, *any* diluent, and *any* addition of aromatic flavoring, and you have one instantly. What puzzles me is how this massive fact, so revolutionary in human history and so conducive to human happiness, jumped so quickly from New Orleans to the Hudson Valley. It seems much more likely that the *cocktail* was actually known and esteemed in the Albany region some time before Peychaud shook up his first Sazerac on the lower Mississippi. But, lacking precise proof to this effect, I am glad to give that Mousterian soda jerker full faith and credit, and to greet him with huzzas for his service to humanity.

Cocktails are now so numerous that no bartender, however talented, can remember how to make all of them, or even the half of them. In the "Savoy Cocktail Book," published in 1930, the number listed is nearly seven hundred, and in the "Bartender's Guide," by Trader Vic, published in 1947, it goes beyond sixteen hundred. No man short of a giant could try them all, and nine-tenths of them, I believe, would hardly be worth trying. The same

sound instinct that prompts the more enlightened minority
of mankind to come in out of a thunderstorm has also
taught it to confine its day-in-and-day-out boozing to
about a dozen standard varieties—the *Martini*, the
Manhattan, the *Daiquiri*, the *Side Car*, the *Orange Blossom*,
the *Alexander*, the *Bronx*, and a few others. The lexicogra-
pher John Russell Bartlett, in the fourth edition of his
"Dictionary of Americanisms," 1877, also listed the *Jersey*
and the *Japanese*, but neither survives except in the bartenders' guides, which no bartender ever reads. The
"Dictionary of American English" traces the *Manhattan*
only to 1894, but that is absurd, for I saw a justice of the
Supreme Court of the United States drink one in a
Washington barroom in 1886. The others that I have mentioned, save the *Martini* and the *Bronx*, are not listed in
any dictionary at hand, though millions of them go down
the esophagi of one-hundred-per-cent Americans every
week, and maybe every day. A correspondent tells me that
the *Daiquiri* was invented by American engineers
marooned at Daiquiri, near Santiago de Cuba, in 1898;
they ran out of whiskey and gin but found a large supply
of pale Cuban rum, and got it down by mixing it with
lime juice. The origin of the *Martini* is quite unknown to
science, though I have heard the suggestion that its name
comes from that of Martin Luther. The origin of the *Bronx*
ditto; all that is known is that it preceded the *Bronx Cheer*.
The origin of the *Alexander* ditto, despite some fancy
theories. The *Old-fashioned* is supposed to be the grandfather of them all, and it really may be, for its formula
greatly resembles that of the Hudson *Balance* cocktail of
1806, but the fact remains that Bartlett did not mention it
in 1877 and that it is not to be found in any earlier reference works, not even the *Congressional Globe*, predecessor
of the *Congressional Record*.

Some time ago, the St. Louis *Post-Dispatch*, a high-toned paper, dug up a local historian who testified that the *highball* was named by Lilburn McNair, a grandson of the first governor of Missouri and a shining light of St. Louis bar society in the nineties. It seems to be true that the name was first heard about that time, for *highball* was never applied before to a mixture of rye or bourbon and soda or tap water, and Scotch whiskey did not come upon the American market until the early nineties. (My father, trying his first shot of it in 1894, carried on in a violent manner, and died, four years later, believing that it was made by quack saloonkeepers in their cellars, of creosote and sweet spirits of nitre.) But there are old-timers in Boston who say that the first *highball* was shoved across the bar at the Parker House there, and the late Patrick Gavin Duffy, an eminent bartender of New York, claimed in his "The Official Mixer's Manual" that he borned it at the old Ashland House in 1895. Why the name? Most of the authorities say that it arose from the fact that the bartenders of the nineties called a glass a *ball* and that *highball* flowed naturally from the fact that what was formerly a whiskey-and-soda needed a taller glass than a straight whiskey. But all the bartenders above eighty that I am acquainted with say that *ball* was never used for a glass. Other authorities report that *highball* was lifted from the railroad men, who use the term for go ahead. But this sounds pretty thin, for if the railroad men of that era had ever detected a bartender putting water (and especially soda water) into whiskey, they would have butchered him on the spot. Thus the matter stands. I pant for light, but there is no light.

The history of *Mickey Finn* is equally murky. Herbert Asbury says, in his "Gem of the Prairie," a history of the rise of culture in Chicago, that the name was borrowed from that of a Chicago saloon keeper who had been a lush-roller in his early days and operated a college for pickpockets in connection with his saloon. The patrons of the place were a somewhat mischievous lot, and not infrequently Finn had to go to the aid of his bouncer. They used the side arms in vogue at the time—to wit, bung starters, shillelaghs, joints of gas pipe, and lengths of garden hose filled with BB shot—but the work was laborious, and Finn longed for something sneakier and slicker. One day, a colored swami named Hall offered to mix him a dose that would knock out the friskiest patient in a few minutes. The formula turned out to be half an ounce of chloral hydrate in a double slug of pseudo-whiskey. It worked so well that many of those to whom it was given landed in the morgue, and Finn was so pleased with it that he gave it his name. I have a very high opinion of Asbury's lexicographical and sociological parts, but I am still waiting to hear him explain how *Mickey Finn* became transferred from a dose comparable to an atomic bomb to a drink of bathtub gin with a drop or two of croton oil in it—a mixture that certainly got rid of the customer but did him no more permanent harm than a draught of Glauber's salts. Also, I am waiting to hear from him why a Chicago saloon keeper had to wait for a colored necromancer to tell him about *knockout drops,* which had been familiar in American criminal circles since the first Grant administration. My own great-uncle, Julius by name, got a massive shot of them in Wheeling, West Virginia, in 1870, and was never the same man afterward.

These few examples reveal the pitfalls, booby traps, and other difficulties that strew the path of anyone seriously interested in the origin and history of booze terms. The dictionaries, always prissy, avoid most of them as they avoid the immemorial four-letter words. You will not find *Mickey Finn* in the great Webster of 1934, or in the "Dictionary of American English," or in the "Supplement to the New English Dictionary." It appears, to be sure, in some of the newer and smaller dictionaries, but almost always with the equivocal definition of "a drugged drink." So far as I have been able to discover, only "Words: The New Dictionary," brought out in 1947, says that its essential medicament is a cathartic, not a narcotic. Even Berrey and Van den Bark, in their invaluable "American Thesaurus of Slang," 1942, are content to list it under the rubric of *strong liquor,* along with *forty-rod, pop-skull,* and *third rail,* though I should add that they note that tramps and criminals now use it to designate any laxative victual. *Highball* is listed in nearly all the dictionaries published since 1930, but not one of them attempts its etymology. Nor does any of them try to unravel the mystery of *cocktail.*

[1948]

FEAR OF FLYING

Erica Jong

Growing up female in America. What a liability! You grew up with your ears full of cosmetic ads, love songs, advice columns, whoreoscopes, Hollywood gossip, and moral dilemmas on the level of TV soap operas. What litanies the advertisers of the good life chanted at you! What curious catechisms!

"Be kind to your behind." "Blush like you mean it." "Love your hair." "Want a better body? We'll rearrange the one you've got." "That shine on your face should come from him, not from your skin." "You've come a long way, baby." "How to score with every male in the zodiac." "The stars and sensual you." "To a man they say Cutty Sark." "A diamond is forever." "If you're concerned about douching . . ." "Length and coolness come together." "How I solved my intimate odor problem." "Lady be cool." "Every woman alive loves Chanel No. 5." "What makes a shy girl get intimate?" "*Femme,* we named it after you."

What all the ads and all the whoreoscopes seemed to imply was that if only you were narcissistic *enough,* if only you took proper care of your smells, your hair, your boobs, your eyelashes, your armpits, your crotch, your stars, your scars, and your choice of Scotch in bars—you would meet a beautiful, powerful, potent, and rich man who would satisfy every longing, fill every hole, make your heart skip a beat (or stand still), make you misty, and fly you to the moon (preferably on gossamer wings), where you would live totally satisfied forever.

And the crazy part of it was that even if you were *clever,*
even if you spent your adolescence reading John Donne
and Shaw, even if you studied history or zoology or
physics and hoped to spend your life pursuing some
difficult and challenging career—you *still* had a mind
full of all the soupy longings that every high-school
girl was awash in. It didn't matter, you see, whether
you had an IQ of 170 or an IQ of 70, you were brain-
washed all the same. Only the surface trappings were
different. Only the *talk* was a little more sophisticated.
Underneath it all, you longed to be annihilated by love,
to be swept off your feet, to be filled up by a giant prick
spouting sperm, soapsuds, silks and satins, and of course,
money. Nobody bothered to tell you what marriage
was really about. You weren't even provided, like
European girls, with a philosophy of cynicism and prac-
ticality. You expected *not* to desire any other men after
marriage. And you expected your husband not to desire
any other women. Then the desires came and you were
thrown into a panic of self-hatred. What an evil woman
you were! How could you keep being infatuated with
strange men? How could you study their bulging trousers
like that? How could you sit at a meeting imagining how
every man in the room would screw? How could you
sit on a train fucking total strangers with your eyes?
How could you *do* that to your husband? Did anyone
ever tell you that maybe it had nothing whatever to do
with your husband?

And what about those other longings which marriage
stifled? Those longings to hit the open road from time to
time, to discover whether you could still live alone inside
your own head, to discover whether you could manage
to survive in a cabin in the woods without going mad; to
discover, in short, whether you were still whole after so

many years of being half of something (like the back two legs of a horse outfit on the vaudeville stage).

Five years of marriage had made me itchy for all those things: itchy for men, and itchy for solitude. Itchy for sex and itchy for the life of a recluse. I knew my itches were contradictory—and that made things even worse. I knew my itches were un-American—and that made things *still* worse. It is heresy in America to embrace any way of life except as half of a couple. Solitude is un-American. It may be condoned in a man—especially if he is a "glamorous bachelor" who "dates starlets" during a brief interval between marriages. But a woman is always presumed to be alone as a result of abandonment, not choice. And she is treated that way: as a pariah. There is simply no dignified way for a woman to live alone. Oh, she can get along financially perhaps (though not nearly as well as a man), but emotionally she is never left in peace. Her friends, her family, her fellow workers never let her forget that her husbandlessness, her childlessness, her *selfishness,* in short— is a reproach to the American way of life.

Even more to the point: the woman (unhappy though she knows her married friends to be) can never let *herself* alone. She lives as if she were constantly on the brink of some great fulfillment. As if she were waiting for Prince Charming to take her away "from all this." All what? The solitude of living inside her own soul? The certainty of being herself instead of half of something else?

My response to all this was not (not yet) to have an affair and not (not yet) to hit the open road, but to evolve my fantasy of the Zipless Fuck. The zipless fuck was more than a fuck. It was a platonic ideal. Zipless because when you came together zippers fell away like rose petals, underwear blew off in one breath like dandelion fluff. Tongues intertwined and turned liquid. Your whole soul flowed out through your tongue and into the mouth of your lover.

For the true, ultimate zipless A-1 fuck, it was necessary that you never get to know the man very well. I had noticed, for example, how all my infatuations dissolved as soon as I really became friends with a man, became sympathetic to his problems, listened to him *kvetch* about his wife, or ex-wives, his mother, his children. After that I would like him, perhaps even love him—but without passion. And it was passion that I wanted. I had also learned that a sure way to exorcise an infatuation was to write about someone, to observe his tics and twitches, to anatomize his personality in type. After that he was an insect on a pin, a newspaper clipping laminated in plastic. I might enjoy his company, even admire him at moments, but he no longer had the power to make me wake up trembling in the middle of the night. I no longer dreamed about him. He had a face.

So another condition for the zipless fuck was brevity. And anonymity made it even better.

During the time I lived in Heidelberg I commuted to Frankfurt four times a week to see my analyst. The ride took an hour each way and trains became an important part of my fantasy life. I kept meeting beautiful men on the train, men who barely spoke English, men whose clichés and banalities were hidden by my ignorance of French, or Italian, or even German. Much as I had to admit it, there are *some* beautiful men in Germany.

One scenario of the zipless fuck was perhaps inspired by an Italian movie I saw years ago. As time went by, I embellished it to suit my head. It used to play over and over again as I shuttled back and forth from Heidelberg to Frankfurt, from Frankfurt to Heidelberg:

•

A grimy European train compartment (Second Class). The seats are leatherette and hard. There is a sliding door to the corridor outside. Olive trees rush by the window. Two Sicilian peasant women sit together on one side with a child between them. They appear to be mother and grandmother and granddaughter. Both women vie with each other to stuff the little girl's mouth with food. Across the way (in the window seat) is a pretty young widow in a heavy black veil and a tight black dress which reveals her voluptuous figure. She is sweating profusely and her eyes are puffy. The middle seat is empty. The corridor seat is occupied by an enormously fat woman with a moustache. Her huge haunches cause her to occupy almost half of the vacant center seat. She is reading a pulp romance in which the characters are photographed models and the dialogue appears in little puffs of smoke above their heads.

This fivesome bounces along for a while, the widow and the fat woman keeping silent, the mother and grandmother talking to the child and each other about the food. And then the train screeches to a halt in a town called (perhaps) CORLEONE. A tall languid-looking soldier, unshaven, but with a beautiful mop of hair, a cleft chin, and somewhat devilish, lazy eyes, enters the compartment, looks insolently around, sees the empty half-seat between the fat woman and the widow, and, with many flirtatious apologies, sits down. He is sweaty and disheveled but basically a gorgeous hunk of flesh, only slightly rancid from the heat. The train screeches out of the station.

•

Then we become aware only of the bouncing of the train and the rhythmic way the soldier's thighs are rubbing against the thighs of the widow. Of course, he is also rubbing against the haunches of the fat lady—and she is trying to move away from him—which is quite unnecessary because he is unaware of her haunches. He is watching the large gold cross between the widow's breasts swing back and forth in her deep cleavage. Bump. Pause. Bump. It hits one moist breast and then another. It seems to hesitate in between as if paralyzed between two repelling magnets. The pit and the pendulum. He is hypnotized. She stares out the window, looking at each olive tree as if she had never seen olive trees before. He rises awkwardly, half-bows to the ladies, and struggles to open the window. When he sits down again his arm accidentally grazes the widow's belly. She appears not to notice. He rests his left hand on the seat between his thigh and hers and begins to wind rubber fingers around and under the soft flesh of her thigh. She continues staring at each olive tree as if she were God and had just made them and were wondering what to call them.

Meanwhile the enormously fat lady is packing away her pulp romance in an iridescent green plastic string bag full of smelly cheeses and blackening bananas. And the grandmother is rolling ends of salami in greasy newspaper. The mother is putting on the little girl's sweater and wiping her face with a handkerchief, lovingly moistened with maternal spittle. The train screeches to a stop in a town called (perhaps) PRIZZI, and the fat lady, the mother, the grandmother, and the little girl leave the compartment. Then the train begins to move again. The gold cross begins to bump, pause, bump between the widow's moist breasts, the fingers begin to curl under the widow's thighs, the widow continues to stare at the olive trees. Then the fingers are sliding between her thighs and they are parting her thighs, and they are moving upward into the fleshy gap between her heavy black stockings and her garters, and they are sliding up under her garters into the damp unpantied place between her legs.

The train enters a *galleria,* or tunnel, and in the semidarkness the symbolism is consummated.

There is the soldier's boot in the air and the dark walls of the tunnel and the hypnotic rocking of the train and the long high whistle as it finally emerges.

Wordlessly, she gets off at a town called, perhaps, BIVONA. She crosses the tracks, stepping carefully over them in her narrow black shoes and heavy black stockings. He stares after her as if he were Adam wondering what to name her. Then he jumps up and dashes out of the train in pursuit of her. At that very moment a long freight train pulls through the parallel track obscuring his view and blocking his way. Twenty-five freight cars later, she has vanished forever.

One scenario of the zipless fuck.
Zipless, you see, *not* because European men have button-flies rather than zipper-flies, and not because the participants are so devastatingly attractive, but because the incident has all the swift compression of a dream and is

seemingly free of all remorse and guilt; because there is no talk of her late husband or of his fiancée; because there is no rationalizing; because there is no talk at *all*. The zipless fuck is absolutely pure. It is free of ulterior motives. There is no power game. The man is not "taking" and the woman is not "giving." No one is attempting to cuckold a husband or humiliate a wife. No one is trying to prove anything or get anything out of anyone. The zipless fuck is the purest thing there is. And it is rarer than the unicorn. And I have never had one. Whenever it seemed I was close, I discovered a horse with a papier-mâché horn, or two clowns in a unicorn suit. Alessandro, my Florentine friend, came close. But he was, after all, one clown in a unicorn suit.

Consider this tapestry, my life.

[1973]

HOW TO CUT DOWN ON DRINKING AND SMOKING QUITE SO MUCH

L. Rust Hills

The trouble with most advice you get about smoking and drinking is that it comes from the wrong people. It's people who have somehow managed to quit smoking entirely who are only too willing to tell you how they did it and how you ought to too. It's the alcoholics who couldn't handle booze at all who are always trying to tell you you have to give it up entirely. Their solution is worse than your problem. You don't want to *stop* smoking and drinking, you just want to stop smoking and drinking *so much*.

Cutting down is a good idea, then, because it's the best way of assuring that you won't have to stop. No drinker wants to have to give up drinking. And smokers feel the same way. Lung cancer is a terrible thing (my father died of it), and early death from emphysema or heart trouble doesn't sound too good either, but a life without cigarettes for your average smoker would appear to be the way the unexamined life was for the Greeks: not worth living.

Some smokers say the only reason to *eat* is how good a cigarette tastes afterward. People who drink can't imagine having a cup of coffee without a cigarette. Life is (I have been known to say) a Three-Legged Stool, supported by Booze, Coffee, and Smokes, which interdepend essentially. Kick away any leg of the stool and the whole old corpus comes crashing to the kitchen floor.

One good thing about drinking (besides how it makes you feel) is that it is legal and socially acceptable more or less everywhere. In this, it is just about unique—except for sex, which is different—among all the euphoria-producing things, but there's an underestimated aspect to smoking, too, one that's very singular in this dislocated modern society where we're all made restless and anxious by a lot of hidden desires and aimless longings. Longing for a cigarette is one of the least aimless longings there is. Cigarettes create their own recognizable desire *and* the means of fulfilling it.

Several years ago I was bitten three times by two wasps (different pairs of them, of course) about six months apart, each time with a fantastically worse reaction. The third time I nearly died. I thought I'd had a heart attack. Coming finally out of the anaphylactic shock or whatever it's called—believe me, it's like *coming* back from the dead—well, coming back from the dead, the first thing I wanted was my sense of humor back and when I saw I'd got that the next thing I wanted, the *first* thing I wanted after I saw I was alive, was a cigarette. Dr. Haliday, who had rushed over to give me the adrenaline shot that brought me back (since gone to the grave himself), had given up smoking about six months before, but he breathed a great sigh and had a cigarette with me. Some people, if they died of *lung cancer* and then somehow managed to come back to life, what they'd want first is a cigarette.

They couldn't imagine taking a break in their work—for coffee or just for a rest—if they couldn't have a cigarette. There's no point in stopping at all, no point in even *doing* a job, much less doing it *right,* unless when you're through you can reward yourself with a cigarette.

But the "reward" idea is one of our main troubles with smoking and drinking. When the work's going well you think you "deserve" to smoke as much as you want. After a long hard day of good work at the office you deserve to unwind with a few drinks. After a long hard week, you feel you deserve to get drunk on Friday night. All that's true: you *do* deserve it. But ultimately so much self-rewarding becomes self-punishing. Feeling lousy all weekend is the reward you get for your hard week's work. It doesn't seem fair, I know; and if I were God I'd make it that people would never get hangovers unless they didn't deserve to get drunk. I would do that for you, but I can't.

It also may be that you drink and smoke so much because you like it: you like the feeling that a drink, or a lot of drinks, gives you; and while you may not exactly *like* the feeling a cigarette gives you, you sure as hell *don't* like the feeling you get when you haven't had one for an hour or two; also, you may actually like the taste of tobacco and liquor. But the real reason you drink and smoke so much is that you still have the idea, formed somewhere way back when, that smoking and drinking too much is really a very romantic thing to do. It seems very grown-up to you if you are young, and it seems very youthful to you if you are old.

In his autobiography, Lincoln Steffens describes his romance with drinking:

> Once, for example, as I staggered (a little more than I had to) away from the bar, I overheard one man say to another: "Those boys can carry some liquor, can't they?"
>
> That was great. But better still was the other loafer's reply: "Yes," he said, "but it's tough to see young men setting out on the downgrade to hell that way."

The romantic idea that one has a brilliant future somehow being ruined by drinking is natural to a college sophomore, but it ought to be abandoned in maturity. The trouble is it remains in the subconscious, sneakily invidious, so that even the ugly hangover becomes glamorous. When I was young and seldom got hangovers, or not bad ones, I'd often pretend to be in a very bad way "the morning after." It made for a lot of companionable talk in college about the "hair of the dog" and getting "a quick one." Drugs— which come complete with that great language about "turning on" and "highs" and "freaking out" and "coming down" and so on—must seem equivalently dangerous and romantic. Years and years later, when stupid pride in a hangover was replaced by sensible shame on a number of occasions, when for various reasons I tried to conceal how my hands were trembling, I remember even then having that invidious secret sense of how romantic it was that I was in such a bad way and actually trying to conceal it.

It's in our earliest, most impressionable youth that we learn how romantic it is to be dissolute. I remember how we used to hang around Lou Berry's stationery store in Williston Park endlessly discussing Wilbur Slaymacher, a stunted unattractive kid we all admired because all he ever had for breakfast was a Coke and a coffin nail. Once you have come to the realization that Wilbur Slaymacher, "setting out on the downgrade to hell that way," as Lincoln Steffens puts it, despite the key fact that there was nothing else to recommend him at all, is nevertheless a *genuinely romantic figure,* once you grasp that, in late childhood or early adolescence, it is something (a lesson learned, or something) that you never ever get over. It is with you the rest of your life, this misconception.

Oh, let me tell you this example of how romantic smoking and drinking can seem to be. When I came home from Europe determined to straighten myself out, I went to *Esquire* looking for a job, and there in this big Madison Avenue office were Frederick A. Birmingham, The Editor, and Leonard Wallace Robinson, The Managing Editor, and they were talking dirty and kidding around with Imie Camelli, The Secretary, and were real slick and smooth, but easy about it somehow; and then FAB said he had an eleven-thirty appointment with his dentist and then a lunch date with George Frazier or Leslie Saalberg or someone elegant like that, and he and Len got to joking about how when you had a martini after having novocaine you could only feel one side of the glass and when you ate the olive you could only taste half of it. It doesn't seem very funny now, but God did it seem marvelous then. I had no job, no apartment, dwindling money, my father was dying of you-know-what and my mother was a real problem, there was a heat wave, I had poison ivy, terrible athlete's foot, bleeding gums from trenchmouth, had just gotten divorced, and for the first (and probably last) time in my life I thought New York City was great. Maybe it was the idea of an expense-account lunch. But I think what seemed so romantic and great was having to have your martinis at lunch even though your mouth was shot full of novocaine.

It's no use trying to point out the horrors of smoking, even to young people today. All you do is contribute to the creation of more Wilbur Slaymacher figures. Danger is romantic, and at that age sickness and death seem very far away. The more horrible the facts and statistics that come out about smoking, the more attractive it seems to be to a certain kind of normal irrational adolescent mentality—that is, most of the kids and virtually all of the adults I know.

One of the ways to cut down is to work a kind of jujitsu on this crazy secret conviction. Get it in your mind that cutting down is really *just* as romantic. Instead of confessing (really boasting) about how much you drink and smoke, confess-boast about how much you *used* to drink and smoke. "Boy, I *had* to cut down," you can say. "I was slowly killing myself."

The actual methods you use to cut down aren't as important as getting your mind right about it. The basic idea is that you limit yourself in certain specific arbitrary ways. You can set a limit on how many you'll smoke each day—say ten or fifteen or even thirty—and count them out each morning into the elegant silver case you got from your grandfather or a junk store.

The system gets thrown off when someone disastrously bums a cigarette from you, but then there's joy when someone offers you one of his, an extra you don't have to count.

A scheme that worked awhile for me was writing down a *reason* for every cigarette I had: "work break," "before lunch," "after lunch," "need to reconsider what done so far," and so on. When I found myself writing down ten reasons *in advance* one afternoon so that I could just go ahead and smoke whenever I wanted, I gave the system up.

All these systems eventually break down: that may be in the nature of using system as a process of personal reform. You're interested in the system for a while; then you get impatient with it. The thing to do then is switch to another. I'll admit a system isn't much of a *system* when you're switching from one to another all the time. But it's what you have to do, all you *can* do.

I had one hell of a system once for cutting down on drinking so much. I was sharing a big summer house with a lot of city people, and I came to realize I'd been getting bombed every night. I was there all the time; the others would come up just weekends or on their vacations. Anyway, I devised this incredibly clever system: the idea was, I'd plan ahead just exactly what I would do drinking-wise for each and every day of a four-day cycle. On what became known as A First Day, I wouldn't drink at all—

nothing, not a single drink. This was to prove I wasn't an alcoholic and could do without it. On the next day, A Second Day, I would have one drink before dinner and one drink after dinner—that's all, no more, no matter how often they told me I was a no-fun person. This was to prove I could drink abstemiously, if that isn't a contradiction in terms. On A Third Day, I'd allow myself to drink what I called "moderately." This was to prove I could drink moderately. And on A Fourth Day, it was all-out, anything goes, as much as I wanted. This was to prove I was still a fun person. Then it would be A First Day again. And so on.

Well, the system really did sort of work for a while, but there were difficulties with it, as I guess you must have imagined there would be. On A First Day, after A Fourth Day debauch, is of course just when you need a drink most, at least one drink, if not just one drink before dinner then at least one drink just before bed. On A First Day I'd be irascible all day and go to bed early and not be able to sleep. A Second Day was all right, nothing to get excited about, but the way sensible people live regularly, I guess. A Third Day was always a problem, because my idea of "moderately" kept changing as the evening wore on. A Fourth Day, of course, was just the normal disaster.

One of the main problems of the system was the four-day cycle when everyone else was more or less on a seven-day week. I can't for the life of me remember how I decided on four days or why on earth I didn't change when I saw it wasn't working. If my Fourth Day were to come, say, on the others' Tuesday, there wouldn't be anyone to drink with me; it was awful having A Fourth Day go to waste like that. Then, others couldn't keep track of what day mine was. They'd prolong the cocktail hour unconscionably on A Second Day that happened to be their Friday night. Or I'd be moderately having a couple of drinks on A Third Day, maybe weaving a little as I told a long-winded story, maybe making myself one more at the same time, and I'd overhear one of the householders ask another, "Say, is this A Fourth Day, or what?"

Toward the end, I began switching my days around to accommodate, like a good householder, so *my* good days would coincide with *their* good days. Thus on A Second Day Saturday night, I'd decide during cocktails to have my Second Day tomorrow and my Third Day today; then later in the evening I'd decide to make today my Fourth Day and have my Third Day tomorrow and have my Second Day after that. But things tended to get confused, and of course the First and Second Days got kind of lost, and pretty soon every day was A Fourth Day again. It's really hard to organize systems when you're sharing with others.

But good planning is still really the central secret in cutting down. Good planning features (or *would* feature, if one could ever work things out right) each cigarette and each drink as a pleasant event occurring routinely in the course of a well-ordered day. You would have your first cigarette with your second cup of coffee after you've finished your breakfast. You would have your second when you took your coffee break. Then if you take a glass of sherry before lunch you have another cigarette then. And so on, through a prescheduled, *ordered* day.

So there should be a sense of occasion for having your drinks. I don't for heaven's sake mean a party or anything like that. There's nothing worse than a party for making you forget you're having your drink! No, I mean like a particular time of day to have it, or them. If you're only having two or three you'll want to make them good big strong ones with some punch to them, so you'll *know* you're having them. Nice brown drinks. Certainly you'll want one, or two, before dinner. Maybe you'll want one before lunch, or a glass of wine with lunch (counts one half); and maybe you like to take a nice scotch on the rocks upstairs to bed with you? That's fine as long as it's not a TUD—although for some reason, the TUD is the best drink of the day. "TUD" is an acronym for that Totally Unnecessary Drink, the so-called nightcap, as used in fond phrasing like this: "I think I'll just make this last little Tuddy to take up with me to Lily White's party."

A good way of creating a proper sense of occasion about drinks is to have a different kind of drink for each of the different occasions. I mean, if you go through life never having anything but Johnnie Walker Red Label and water, the only difference between your drinks is the time of day you have them. My parents always had, every night before dinner, either a martini or a manhattan. "Which did we have last night?" one of them would say, and then, "Well, let's have the other, then," or "Oh, let's have it again tonight anyway." A manhattan is a much underrated drink: it *is* kind of sticky and you certainly wouldn't want it every night or even every other night; but it is a cheerful drink, and if it is cold and bleak (the weather, I mean) and you wish you had an open fire, a manhattan is good, perhaps because the cherry in it has some of the same bright warm color. Martinis give you a headache, as everyone knows; but made in a good expensive restaurant there is nothing like them.

Anyway, my theory is that if you enjoy each of your drinks you won't want so many of them. What gets you drunk is thinking that subsequent drinks are going to pick you up the way the first one did, but of course it doesn't work that way.

Drinking to a schedule presents some of the same hazards and delights as smoking a definite, limited number of cigarettes each day. You have to get everything all set and ready so that you realize both that you're having your drink and also that you're appreciating it. Sometimes you forget, or get busy doing something else, or you're talking with somebody and you forget you're having your drink, and you just drink it down, and then you've drunk it and didn't even realize you were having it, much less appreciate it, and that makes you feel as if you'd been cheated out of it, so you want to have another right away to make up for it, and that's bad.

It may really be that routines, schedules, systems, and the general imposition of order on one's self and one's life are ultimately no match for the tendencies toward indulgence, excess, and chaos that are abroad in the land and apparently inherent within. But you do see, don't you, that all the things I've been telling you hang together? An ordered system-schedule *ought* to work, God knows. It takes fully into account your first realization about smoking and drinking—that you feel you "deserve" a drink or smoke as a "reward." And the method accounts for—in fact, utilizes—your second realization—that you think smoking and drinking are romantic—for this is a truly grown-up way to drink and smoke. And your third realization—that the ordered, scheduled life ultimately provides more pleasure (I realize you haven't really *realized* this yet)—will be manifest in the relish with which you appreciate each cigarette and each drink as it becomes available to you in the time scheme you set up. Awful as the waiting is, it's better than giving them up. Needless to say *considerable* anticipation can develop by the time to have the next cigarette or drink comes around.

Say, what *time* is it getting to be?!

[1972]

THE GROUP

Mary McCarthy

Just at first, in the dark hallway, it had given Dottie rather a funny feeling to be tiptoeing up the stairs only two nights after Kay's wedding to a room right across from Harald's old room, where the same thing had happened to Kay. An awesome feeling, really, like when the group all got the curse at the same time; it filled you with strange ideas about being a woman, with the moon compelling you like the tides. All sorts of weird, irrelevant ideas floated through Dottie's head as the key turned in the lock and she found herself, for the first time, alone with a man in his flat. Tonight was midsummer's night, the summer solstice, when maids had given up their treasure to fructify the crops; she had that in background reading for *A Midsummer Night's Dream*. Her Shakespeare teacher had been awfully keen on anthropology and had had them study in Frazer about the ancient fertility rites and how the peasants in Europe, till quite recent times, had lit big bonfires in honor of the Corn Maiden and then lain together in the fields. College, reflected Dottie as the lamp clicked on, had been almost *too* rich an experience. She felt stuffed with interesting thoughts that she could only confide in Mother, not in a man, certainly, who would probably suppose you were barmy if you started telling him about the Corn Maiden when you were just about to lose your virginity. Even the group would laugh if Dottie confessed that she was exactly in the mood for a long, comfy discussion with Dick, who was so frightfully attractive and unhappy and had so much to give.

But the group would never believe, never in a million years, that Dottie Renfrew would come here, to this attic room that smelled of cooking fat, with a man she hardly knew, who made no secret of his intentions, who had been drinking, heavily, and who was evidently not in love with her. When she put it that way, crudely, she could scarcely believe it herself, and the side of her that wanted to talk was still hoping, probably, to gain a little time, the way, she had noticed, she always started a discussion of current events with the dentist to keep him from turning on the drill. Dottie's dimple twinkled. What an odd impression! If the group could hear that!

And yet when It happened, it was not at all what the group or even Mother would have imagined, not a bit sordid or messy, in spite of Dick's being tight. He had been most considerate, undressing her slowly, in a matter-of-fact way, as if he were helping her off with her outdoor things. He took her hat and furs and put them in the closet and then unfastened her dress, bending over the snaps with a funny, concentrated scowl, rather like Daddy's when he was hooking Mother up for a party. Lifting the dress carefully off her, he had glanced at the label and then back at Dottie, as though to match the two, before he carried it, walking very steadily, to the closet and arranged it on a wooden hanger. After that, he folded each garment as he removed it and set it ceremoniously on the armchair, looking each time at the label with a frown between his brows. When her dress was gone, she felt rather faint for a minute, but he left her in her slip, just as they did in the doctor's office, while he took off her shoes and stockings and undid her brassière and girdle and step-ins, so that finally, when he drew her slip over her head, with great pains so as not to muss her hairdo, she was hardly trembling when she stood there in front of him with nothing

on but her pearls. Perhaps it was going to the doctor so
much or perhaps it was Dick himself, so detached and
impersonal, the way they were supposed to be in art class
with the model, that made Dottie brave. He had not
touched her once, all the time he was undressing her,
except by accident, grazing her skin. Then he pinched
each of her full breasts lightly and told her to relax, in just
the tone Dr. Perry used when he was going to give her a
treatment for her sciatica.

He handed her a book of drawings to look at, while he
went into the closet, and Dottie sat there in the armchair,
trying not to listen. With the book in her lap, she studied
the room conscientiously, in order to know Dick better.
Rooms told a lot about a person. It had a skylight and a
big north window and was surprisingly neat for a man;
there was a drawing board with some work on it which
she longed to peek at, a long plain table, like an ironing
table, monk's-cloth curtains, and a monk's-cloth spread on
the single bed. On the chest of drawers was a framed photograph of a blonde woman, very striking, with a short,
severe haircut; that must be "Betty," the wife. Tacked up
on the wall, there was a snapshot that looked like her in
a bathing suit and a number of sketches from the nude,
and Dottie had the sinking feeling that they might be of
Betty too. She had been doing her very best not to let
herself think about love or let her emotions get entangled,
for she knew that Dick would not like it. It was just a
physical attraction, she had been telling herself over and
over, while trying to remain cool and collected despite
the pounding of her blood, but now, suddenly, when it
was too late to retreat, she had lost her *sang-froid* and was
jealous. Worse than that, even, the idea came to her that
Dick was, well, *peculiar.* She opened the book of drawings
on her lap and found more nudes, signed by some modern

artist she had never heard of! She did not know, a second later, just what she had been expecting, but Dick's return was, by contrast, less bad.

He came in wearing a pair of white shorts and carrying a towel, with a hotel's name on it, which he stretched out on the bed, having turned back the covers. He took the book away from her and put it on a table. Then he made Dottie lie down on the towel, telling her to relax again, in a friendly, instructive voice; while he stood for a minute, looking down at her and smiling, with his hands on his hips, she tried to breathe naturally, reminding herself that she had a good figure, and forced a wan, answering smile to her lips. *"Nothing will happen unless you want it, baby."* The words, lightly stressed, told her how scared and mistrustful she must be looking. "I know, Dick," she answered, in a small, weak, grateful voice, making herself use his name aloud for the first time. "Would you like a cigarette?" Dottie shook her head and let it drop back on the pillow. "All right, then?" "All right." As he moved to turn out the light, she felt a sudden harsh thump of excitement, right in *there*, like what had happened to her in the Italian restaurant when he said "Do you want to come home with me?" and fastened his deep, shadowed eyes on her. Now he turned and looked at her steadily again, his hand on the bridge lamp; her own eyes, widening with amazement at the funny feeling she noticed, as if she were on fire, in the place her thighs were shielding, stared at him, seeking confirmation; she swallowed. In reply, he switched off the lamp and came toward her in the dark, unbuttoning his shorts.

That shift gave her an instant in which to be afraid. She had never seen *that* part of a man, except in statuary and once, at the age of six, when she had interrupted Daddy in his bath, but she had a suspicion that it would be something ugly and darkly inflamed, surrounded by coarse hair. Hence, she had been very grateful for being spared the sight of it, which she did not think she could have borne, and she held her breath as the strange body climbed on hers, shrinking. "Open your legs," he commanded, and her legs obediently fell apart. His hand squeezed her down there, rubbing and stroking; her legs fell farther apart, and she started to make weak, moaning noises, almost as if she wanted him to stop. He took his hand away, thank Heaven, and fumbled for a second; then she felt it, the thing she feared, being guided into her as she braced herself and stiffened. "Relax," he whispered. "You're ready." It was surprisingly warm and smooth, but it hurt terribly, pushing and stabbing. "Damn it," he said. "Relax. You're making it harder." Just then, Dottie screamed faintly; it had gone all the way in. He put his hand over her mouth and then settled her legs around him and commenced to move it back and forth inside her. At first, it hurt so that she flinched at each stroke and tried to pull back, but this only seemed to make him more determined. Then, while she was still praying for it to be over, surprise of surprises, she started to like it a little. She got the idea, and her body began to move too in answer, as he pressed *that* home in her slowly, over and over, and slowly drew it back, as if repeating a question. Her breath came quicker. Each lingering stroke, like a violin bow, made her palpitate for the next. Then, all of a sudden, she seemed to explode in a series of long, uncontrollable contractions that embarrassed her, like the hiccups, the moment they were over, for it was as if she had forgotten Dick as a person; and he, as if he sensed this, pulled quickly away from her and thrust that part of himself onto her stomach, where it pushed and pounded at her flesh. Then he too jerked and moaned, and Dottie felt something damp and sticky running down the hill of her belly.

Minutes passed; the room was absolutely still; through the skylight Dottie could see the moon. She lay there, with Dick's weight still on her, suspecting that something had gone wrong—probably her fault. His face was turned sideward so that she could not look into it, and his chest was squashing her breasts so that she could hardly breathe. Both their bodies were wet, and the cold perspiration from him ran down her face and matted her side hair and made a little rivulet between her breasts; on her lips it had a salty sting that reminded her forlornly of tears. She was ashamed of the happiness she had felt. Evidently, he had not found her satisfactory as a partner or else he would say something. Perhaps the woman was not supposed to move? "Damn it," he had said to her, when he was hurting her, in such a testy voice, like a man saying "Damn it, why can't we have dinner on time?" or something unromantic like that. Was it her screaming out that had spoiled everything? Or had she made a *faux pas* at the end, somehow? She wished that books were a little more explicit; Krafft-Ebing, which Kay and Helena had found at a secondhand bookstore and kept reading aloud from, as if it were very funny, mostly described nasty things like men making love to hens, and even then did not explain how it was done. The thought of the blonde on the bureau filled her with hopeless envy; probably Dick at this moment was making bitter comparisons. She could feel his breathing and smell the stale alcohol that came from him in gusts. In the bed, there was a peculiar pungent odor, and she feared that it might come from her.

The horrible idea occurred to her that he had fallen asleep, and she made a few gentle movements to try to extricate herself from under him. Their damp skins, stuck together, made a little sucking noise when she pulled away, but she could not roll his weight off her. Then she knew that he was asleep. Probably he was tired, she said to herself forgivingly; he had those dark rings under his eyes. But down in her heart she knew that he ought not to have gone to sleep like a ton of bricks on top of her; it was the final proof, if she still needed one, that she meant nothing to him. When he woke up tomorrow morning and found her gone, he would probably be glad. Or perhaps he would not even remember who had been there with him; she could not guess how much he had had to drink before he met her for dinner. What had happened, she feared, was that he had simply passed out. She saw that her only hope of saving her own dignity was to dress in the dark and steal away. But she would have to find the bathroom somewhere outside in that unlit hall. Dick began to snore. The sticky liquid had dried and was crusting on her stomach; she felt she could not go back to the Vassar Club without washing it off. Then the worst thought, almost, of all struck her. Supposing he had started to have an emission while he was still inside her? Or if he had used one of the rubber things and it had broken when she had jerked like that and that was why he had pulled so sharply away? She had heard of the rubber things breaking or leaking and how a woman could get pregnant from just a single drop. Full of determination, Dottie heaved and squirmed to free herself, until Dick raised his head in the moonlight and stared at her, without recognition. It was all true then, Dottie thought miserably; he had just gone to sleep and forgotten her. She tried to slide out of the bed.

Dick sat up and rubbed his eyes. "Oh, it's you, Boston," he muttered, putting an arm around her waist. "Forgive me for dropping off." He got up and turned on the bridge lamp. Dottie hurriedly covered herself with the sheet and averted her face; she was still timorous of seeing him in the altogether. "I must go home, Dick," she said soberly, stealing a sideward look at her clothes folded on the armchair. "*Must* you?" he inquired in a mocking tone; she could imagine his reddish eyebrows shooting up. "You needn't trouble to dress and see me downstairs," she went on quickly and firmly, her eyes fixed on the rug where his bare handsome feet were planted. He stooped and picked up his shorts; she watched his feet clamber into them. Then her eyes slowly rose and met his searching gaze. "What's the matter, Boston?" he said kindly. "Girls don't run home, you know, on their first night. Did it hurt you much?" Dottie shook her head. "Are you bleeding?" he demanded. "Come on, let me look." He lifted her up and moved her down on the bed, the sheet trailing along with her; there was a small bloodstain on the towel. "The very bluest," he said, "but only a minute quantity. Betty bled like a pig." Dottie said nothing. "Out with it, Boston," he said brusquely, jerking a thumb toward the framed photograph. "Does *she* put your nose out of joint?" Dottie made a brave negative sign. There was one thing she had to say. "Dick," and she shut her eyes in shame, "do you think I should take a douche?" "A douche?" he repeated in a mystified tone. "Why? What for?" "Well, in case . . . *you* know . . . birth control," murmured Dottie. Dick stared at her and suddenly burst out laughing; he dropped onto a straight chair and threw his handsome head back. "My dear girl," he said, "we just employed the most ancient form of birth control. *Coitus interruptus,* the old Romans called it, and a horrid nuisance it is." "I thought perhaps . . . ?" said Dottie. "Don't think. What did you think? I promise you, there isn't a single sperm swimming up to fertilize your irreproachable ovum. Like the man in the Bible, I spilled my seed on the ground, or, rather, on your very fine belly." With a swift motion, he pulled the sheet back before she could stop him. "Now," he said, "lay bare your thoughts." Dottie shook her head and blushed. Wild horses could not make her, for the words embarrassed her frightfully; she had nearly choked on "douche" and "birth control," as it was. "We must get you cleaned up," he decreed after a moment's silence. He put on a robe and slippers and disappeared to the bathroom. It seemed a long time before he came back, bringing a dampened towel, with which he swabbed off her stomach. Then he dried her, rubbing hard with the dry end of it, sitting down beside her on the bed. He himself appeared much fresher, as though he had washed, and he smelled of mouthwash and tooth powder. He lit two cigarettes and gave her one and settled an ashtray between them.

"You *came*, Boston," he remarked, with the air of a satisfied instructor. Dottie glanced uncertainly at him; could he mean that thing she had done that she did not like to think about? "I beg your pardon," she murmured. "I mean you had an orgasm." Dottie made a vague, still-inquiring noise in her throat; she was pretty sure, now, she understood, but the new word discombobulated her. "A climax," he added, more sharply. "Do they teach that word at Vassar?" "Oh," said Dottie, almost disappointed that that was all there was to it. "Was that . . . ?" She could not finish the question. "That was it," he nodded. "That is, if I am a judge." "It's normal then?" she wanted to know, beginning to feel better. Dick shrugged. "Not for girls of your upbringing. Not the first time, usually. Appearances to the contrary, you're probably highly sexed."

Dottie turned even redder. According to Kay, a climax was something very unusual, something the husband brought about by carefully studying his wife's desires and by patient manual stimulation. The terms made Dottie shudder, even in memory; there was a horrid bit, all in Latin, in Krafft-Ebing, about the Empress Maria Theresa and what the court doctor told her consort to do that Dottie had glanced at quickly and then tried to forget. Yet even Mother hinted that satisfaction was something that came after a good deal of time and experience and that love made a big difference. But when Mother talked about satisfaction, it was not clear exactly what she meant, and Kay was not clear either, except when she quoted from books. Polly Andrews once asked her whether it was the same as feeling passionate when you were necking (that was when Polly was engaged), and Kay said yes, pretty much, but Dottie now thought that Kay had been mistaken or else trying to hide the truth from Polly for some reason. Dottie had felt passionate, quite a few times, when she was dancing with someone terribly attractive, but that was quite different from the thing Dick meant. You would almost think that Kay did not know what she was talking about. Or else that Kay and Mother meant something else altogether and this thing with Dick *was* abnormal. And yet he seemed so pleased, sitting there, blowing out smoke rings; probably, having lived abroad, he knew more than Mother and Kay.

"What are you frowning over now, Boston?" Dottie gave a start. "To be highly sexed," he said gently, "is an excellent thing in a woman. You mustn't be ashamed." He took her cigarette and put it out and laid his hands on her shoulders. "Buck up," he said. "What you're feeling is natural. *'Post coitum, omne animal triste est,'* as the Roman poet said." He slipped his hand down the slope of her shoulder and lightly touched her nipple. "Your body surprised you tonight. You must learn to know it." Dottie nodded. "Soft," he murmured, pressing the nipple between his thumb and forefinger. "Detumescence, that's what you're experiencing." Dottie drew a quick breath, fascinated; her doubts slid away. As he continued to squeeze it, her nipple stood up. "Erectile tissue," he said informatively and touched the other breast. "See," he said, and they both looked downward. The two nipples were hard and full, with a pink aureole of goose pimples around them; on her breasts were a few dark hairs. Dottie waited tensely. A great relief had surged through her; these were the very terms Kay cited from the marriage handbooks. Down there, she felt a quick new tremor. Her lips parted. Dick smiled. "You feel something?" he said. Dottie nodded. "You'd like it again?" he said, assaying her with his hand. Dottie stiffened; she pressed her thighs together. She was ashamed of the violent sensation his exploring fingers had discovered. But he held his hand there, between her clasped thighs, and grasped her right hand in his other, guiding it downward to the opening of his robe and pressed it over that part of himself, which was soft and limp, rather sweet, really, all curled up on itself like a fat worm. Sitting beside her, he looked into her face as he stroked her down there and tightened her hand on him. "There's a little ridge there," he whispered. "Run your fingers up and down it." Dottie obeyed, wonderingly; she felt his organ stiffen a little, which gave her a strange sense of power. She struggled against the excitement his tickling thumb was producing in her own external part; but as she felt him watching her, her eyes closed and her thighs spread open. He disengaged her hand, and she fell back on the bed, gasping. His thumb continued its play and she let herself yield to what it was doing, her whole attention concentrated on a tense pinpoint of sensation, which suddenly discharged itself in a nervous, fluttering spasm; her body arched and heaved and then lay still. When his hand returned to touch her, she struck it feebly away. "Don't," she moaned, rolling over on her stomach. This second climax, which she now recognized from the first one, though it was different, left her jumpy and disconcerted; it was something less thrilling and more like being tickled relentlessly or having to go to the bathroom. "Didn't you like that?" he demanded, turning her head over on the pillow, so that she could not hide herself from him. She hated to think of his having watched her while he brought *that* about. Slowly, Dottie opened her eyes and resolved to tell the truth. "Not quite so much as the other, Dick." Dick laughed. "A nice normal girl. Some of your sex prefer that." Dottie shivered; she could not deny that it had been exciting but it seemed to her almost perverted. He appeared to read her thoughts. "Have you ever done it with a girl, Boston?" He tilted her face so that he could scan it. Dottie reddened. "Heavens, no." "You come like a house afire. How do you account for that?" Dottie said nothing. "Have you ever done it with yourself?" Dottie shook her head violently; the suggestion wounded her. "In your dreams?" Dottie reluctantly nodded. "A little. Not the whole thing." "Rich erotic fantasies of a Chestnut Street virgin," remarked Dick, stretching. He got up and went to the chest of drawers and took out two pairs of pajamas and tossed one of them to Dottie. "Put them on now and go to the bathroom. Tonight's lesson is concluded."

[1954]

THE DRINKING SCHOOL

Art Hoppe

As a concerned parent and outraged citizen, I am concerned and outraged over the drinking problem among
our college youth. Why can't they be more like us?
Instead, there they are, out marching, demonstrating and
otherwise stirring up trouble over the sober political
issues of the day. Their problem, obviously, is they don't
drink enough. I'm glad, therefore, to report this little-
recognized problem is at last getting the recognition it
deserves. A research sociologist, Mr. Ira H. Cisin, says our
colleges should teach students how to drink.

"Drinking," he says, "can be dangerous, and the young
deserve to be instructed in its uses just as they are taught
to swim and drive a car."

Exactly. And as a lifelong expert in the field, I'm naturally applying for a full professorship. Indeed, I've already
drawn up my lecture notes for my first class in Drinking
123a (no prerequisites required).

"Good morning, students. Welcome to Drinking 123a.
Let me begin by warning you this is no snap course. You
may have easily mastered integral calculus, Etruscan epic
poetry and advanced thermodynamics, but you now must
face the greatest challenge of your academic career: learning how to drink.

"The first seemingly overwhelming obstacle you must
surmount in learning to drink alcoholic beverages is that
they don't taste good. Not to the beginner. And my advice
to you on this point is to choose the beverage you dis-

like least. For example, some beginners find they dislike Scotch less than they dislike bourbon, gin or rye. Thus, by mixing twenty-year-old Scotch with ginger ale, soda pop or cherry cough syrup, they find they can get it down with only the very mildest of shudders. Just remember that with liquor, the taste is the thing. And you can avoid it if you really try.

"Now, then, let us turn to the effect alcohol will have on you. It is not true that alcohol merely makes you dizzy. It also makes you stupid. Some improperly motivated students, feeling stupid and dizzy, will quit right there. Don't be a dropout! Persevere and you will be rewarded by becoming completely irresponsible. Not to mention violently ill. Of course, becoming violently ill doesn't sound too pleasant. But actually, you'll find you're so dizzy, stupid and irresponsible at this point that it won't matter a whit. It's the next morning that matters. There's no point describing in advance the sensations you'll feel the next morning. For one thing, they're indescribable. Just keep in mind the legend of Robert Bruce and the spider. And each time you fall flat on your face, pick yourself up and try again.

"The course will also cover such related subjects as dry sweats, cold sweats, headaches, tremors, personal injury suits, the Penal Code and various symptoms of the manic depressive. The final exam will be a simulated cocktail party at which you will be asked to down seven lukewarm martinis while listening to a two-hour speech in Urdu. Now, then, as to delirium tremens . . ."

No, I can't face it. It's a hopeless task, I say, to lead our militant young people to drink—much as it would contribute to peace on our campuses. Let's be tolerant and let them go on getting even more involved in politics. That way, they'll be driven to it.

[1967]

LOLITA

Vladimir Nabokov

The door of the lighted bathroom stood ajar; in addition to that, a skeleton glow came through the Venetian blind from the outside arclights; these intercrossed rays penetrated the darkness of the bedroom and revealed the following situation.

Clothed in one of her old nightgowns, my Lolita lay on her side with her back to me, in the middle of the bed. Her lightly veiled body and bare limbs formed a Z. She had put both pillows under her dark tousled head; a band of pale light crossed her top vertebrae.

I seemed to have shed my clothes and slipped into pajamas with the kind of fantastic instantaneousness which is implied when in a cinematographic scene the process of changing is cut; and I had already placed my knee on the edge of the bed when Lolita turned her head and stared at me through the striped shadows.

Now this was something the intruder had not expected. The whole pill-spiel (a rather sordid affair, *entre nous soit dit*) had had for object a fastness of sleep that a whole regiment would not have disturbed, and here she was staring at me, and thickly calling me "Barbara." Barbara, wearing my pajamas which were much too tight for her, remained poised motionless over the little sleep-talker. Softly, with a hopeless sigh, Dolly turned away, resuming her initial position. For at least two minutes I waited and strained on the brink, like that tailor with his homemade parachute forty years ago when about to jump from the Eiffel Tower. Her faint breathing had the rhythm of sleep. Finally I heaved myself onto my narrow margin of bed, stealthily pulled at the odds and ends of sheets piled up to the south of my stone-cold heels—and Lolita lifted her head and gaped at me.

As I learned later from a helpful pharmaceutist, the purple pill did not even belong to the big and noble family of barbiturates, and though it might have induced sleep in a neurotic who believed it to be a potent drug, it was too mild a sedative to affect for any length of time a wary, albeit weary, nymphet. Whether the Ramsdale doctor was a charlatan or a shrewd old rogue, does not, and did not, really matter. What mattered was that I had been deceived. When Lolita opened her eyes again, I realized that whether or not the drug might work later in the night, the security I had relied upon was a sham one. Slowly her head turned away and dropped onto her unfair amount of pillow. I lay quite still on my brink, peering at her rumpled hair, at the glimmer of nymphet flesh, where half a haunch and half a shoulder dimly showed, and trying to gauge the depth of her sleep by the rate of her respiration. Some time passed, nothing changed, and I decided I might risk getting a little closer to that lovely and maddening glimmer; but hardly had I moved into its warm purlieus than her breathing was suspended, and I had the odious feeling that little Dolores was wide awake and would explode in screams if I touched her with any part of my wretchedness. Please, reader: no matter your exasperation with the tenderhearted, morbidly sensitive, infinitely circumspect hero of my book, do not skip these essential pages! Imagine me; I shall not exist if you do not imagine me; try to discern the doe in me, trembling in the forest of my own iniquity; let's even smile a little. After all, there is no harm in smiling. For instance (I almost wrote "frinstance"), I had no place to rest my head, and a fit of heartburn (they call those fries "French," *grand Dieu!*) was added to my discomfort.

She was again fast asleep, my nymphet, but still I did not dare to launch upon my enchanted voyage. *La Petite Dormeuse ou l'Amant Ridicule.* Tomorrow I would stuff her with those earlier pills that had so thoroughly numbed her mummy. In the glove compartment—or in the Gladstone bag? Should I wait a solid hour and then creep up again? The science of nympholepsy is a precise science. Actual contact would do it in one second flat. An interspace of a millimeter would do it in ten. Let us wait.

There is nothing louder than an American hotel; and, mind you, this was supposed to be a quiet, cozy, old-fashioned, homey place—"gracious living" and all that stuff. The clatter of the elevator's gate—some twenty yards northeast of my head but as clearly perceived as if it were inside my left temple—alternated with the banging and booming of the machine's various evolutions and lasted well beyond midnight. Every now and then, immediately east of my left ear (always assuming I lay on my back, not daring to direct my viler side toward the nebulous haunch of my bed-mate), the corridor would brim with cheerful, resonant and inept exclamations ending in a volley of good-nights. When *that* stopped, a toilet immediately north of my cerebellum took over. It was a manly, energetic, deep-throated toilet, and it was used many times. Its gurgle and gush and long afterflow shook the wall behind me. Then someone in a southern direction was extravagantly sick, almost coughing out his life with his liquor, and his toilet descended like a veritable Niagara, immediately beyond our bathroom. And when finally all the waterfalls had stopped, and the enchanted hunters were sound asleep, the avenue under the window of my insomnia, to the west of my wake—a

staid, eminently residential, dignified alley of huge trees—
degenerated into the despicable haunt of gigantic trucks
roaring through the wet and windy night.

And less than six inches from me and my burning
life, was nebulous Lolita! After a long stirless vigil, my
tentacles moved towards her again, and this time the
creak of the mattress did not awake her. I managed to
bring my ravenous bulk so close to her that I felt the aura
of her bare shoulder like a warm breath upon my cheek.
And then, she sat up, gasped, muttered with insane
rapidity something about boats, tugged at the sheets
and lapsed back into her rich, dark, young uncon-
sciousness. As she tossed, within that abundant flow of
sleep, recently auburn, at present lunar, her arm struck
me across the face. For a second I held her. She freed
herself from the shadow of my embrace—doing this
not consciously, not violently, not with any personal
distaste, but with the neutral plaintive murmur of a child
demanding its natural rest. And again the situation
remained the same: Lolita with her curved spine to
Humbert, Humbert resting his head on his hand and
burning with desire and dyspepsia.

The latter necessitated a trip to the bathroom for a draft
of water which is the best medicine I know in my case,
except perhaps milk with radishes; and when I re-entered
the strange pale-striped fastness where Lolita's old and new
clothes reclined in various attitudes of enchantment on
pieces of furniture that seemed vaguely afloat, my impossible daughter sat up and in clear tones demanded a
drink, too. She took the resilient and cold paper cup in
her shadowy hand and gulped down its contents gratefully,
her long eyelashes pointing cupward, and then, with an
infantile gesture that carried more charm than any carnal
caress, little Lolita wiped her lips against my shoulder. She

fell back on her pillow (I had subtracted mine while she drank) and was instantly asleep again.

I had not dared offer her a second helping of the drug, and had not abandoned hope that the first might still consolidate her sleep. I started to move toward her, ready for any disappointment, knowing I had better wait but incapable of waiting. My pillow smelled of her hair. I moved toward my glimmering darling, stopping or retreating every time I thought she stirred or was about to stir. A breeze from wonderland had begun to affect my thoughts, and now they seemed couched in italics, as if the surface reflecting them were wrinkled by the phantasm of that breeze. Time and again my consciousness folded the wrong way, my shuffling body entered the sphere of sleep, shuffled out again, and once or twice I caught myself drifting into a melancholy snore. Mists of tenderness enfolded mountains of longing. Now and then it seemed to me that the enchanted prey was about to meet halfway the enchanted hunter, that her haunch was working its way toward me under the soft sand of a remote and fabulous beach; and then her dimpled dimness would stir, and I would know she was farther away from me than ever.

If I dwell at some length on the tremors and gropings of that distant night, it is because I insist upon proving that I am not, and never was, and never could have been, a brutal scoundrel. The gentle and dreamy regions through which I crept were the patrimonies of poets—*not* crime's prowling ground. Had I reached my goal, my ecstasy would have been all softness, a case of internal combustion of which she would hardly have felt the heat, even if she were wide awake. But I still hoped she might gradually be engulfed in a completeness of stupor that would allow me to taste more than a glimmer of her. And so, in between tentative approximations, with a confusion of perception metamorphosing her into eyespots of moonlight or a fluffy flowering bush, I would dream I regained consciousness, dream I lay in wait.

In the first antemeridian hours there was a lull in the restless hotel night. Then around four the corridor toilet cascaded and its door banged. A little after five a reverberating monologue began to arrive, in several installments, from some courtyard or parking place. It was not really a monologue, since the speaker stopped every few seconds to listen (presumably) to another fellow, but that other voice did not reach me, and so no real meaning could be derived from the part heard. Its matter-of-fact intonations, however, helped to bring in the dawn, and the room was already suffused with lilac gray, when several industrious toilets went to work, one after the other, and the clattering and whining elevator began to rise and take down early risers and downers, and for some minutes I miserably dozed, and Charlotte was a mermaid in a greenish tank, and somewhere in the passage Dr. Boyd said "Good morning to you" in a fruity voice, and birds were busy in the trees, and then Lolita yawned.

Frigid gentlewomen of the jury! I had thought that months, perhaps years, would elapse before I dared to reveal myself to Dolores Haze; but by six she was wide awake, and by six fifteen we were technically lovers. I am going to tell you something very strange: it was she who seduced me.

Upon hearing her first morning yawn, I feigned handsome profiled sleep. I just did not know what to do. Would she be shocked at finding me by her side, and not in some spare bed? Would she collect her clothes and lock herself up in the bathroom? Would she demand to be taken at once to Ramsdale—to her mother's bedside—back to camp? But my Lo was a sportive lassie. I felt her eyes on me, and when she uttered at last that beloved chortling note of hers, I knew her eyes had been laughing. She rolled over to my side, and her warm brown hair came against my collarbone. I gave a mediocre imitation of waking up. We lay quietly. I gently caressed her hair, and we gently kissed. Her kiss, to my delirious embarrassment, had some rather comical refinements of flutter and probe which made me conclude she had been coached at an early age by a little Lesbian. No Charlie boy could have taught her *that*. As if to see whether I had my fill and learned the lesson, she drew away and surveyed me. Her cheekbones were flushed, her full underlip glistened, my dissolution was near. All at once, with a burst of rough glee (the sign of the nymphet!), she put her mouth to my ear—but for quite a while my mind could not separate into words the hot thunder of her whisper, and she laughed, and brushed the hair off her face, and tried again, and gradually the odd sense of living in a brand new, mad new dream world, where everything was permissible, came over me as I realized what she was suggesting. I answered I did not know what game she and Charlie had played. "You mean you have never—?"—her features twisted into a stare of disgusted incredulity. "You have never—" she started again. I took time out by nuzzling her a little. "Lay off, will you," she said with a twangy whine, hastily removing her brown shoulder from my lips. (It was very curious the way she considered—and kept doing so for a long time—all caresses except kisses on the mouth or the stark act of love either "romantic slosh" or "abnormal.")

"You mean," she persisted, now kneeling above me, "you never did it when you were a kid?"

"Never," I answered quite truthfully.

"Okay," said Lolita, "here is where we start."

However, I shall not bore my learned readers with a detailed account of Lolita's presumption. Suffice it to say that not a trace of modesty did I perceive in this beautiful hardly formed young girl whom modern co-education, juvenile mores, the campfire racket and so forth had utterly and hopelessly depraved. She saw the stark act merely as part of a youngster's furtive world, unknown to adults. What adults did for purposes of procreation was no business of hers. My life was handled by little Lo in an energetic, matter-of-fact manner as if it were an insensate gadget unconnected with me. While eager to impress me with the world of tough kids, she was not quite prepared for certain discrepancies between a kid's life and mine. Pride alone prevented her from giving up; for, in my strange predicament, I feigned supreme stupidity and had her have her way—at least while I could still bear it. But really these are irrelevant matters; I am not concerned with so-called "sex" at all. Anybody can imagine those elements of animality. A greater endeavor lures me on: to fix once for all the perilous magic of nymphets.

[1955]

SINS OF THE GREEN DEATH

Eve Babitz

I got deflowered on two cans of Rainier Ale when I was 17. It's a local product sold up and down the Coast originating in Seattle (where Mt. Rainier is) and in those days a small can cost about 26 cents. So all this time a handsome, flashy young man had been pouring Courvoisier and champagne into me only to become the tool, in the end, of a can and a half of Rainier Ale. He'd pursued me, done everything—told me he loved me in 8 different languages, introduced me to café society and movie stars, covered me in gardenias and telephoned me 4 times a day, besides which he had a convertible and was rich and had tawny curly hair. It was the Rainier Ale that did it, though, and in the end he became just a pawn of the fancy properties known to exist by coastal natives who have always called this special liquid "The Green Death."

They'd told me I would bleed and it would hurt and it would turn me into a woman. But it didn't hurt. I didn't bleed, and instead of turning into a mature person, I began to wonder what else there was out there that was like Rainier Ale.

At the time, I was trying to shorten my stay at Hollywood High by skipping a grade so that I graduated in summer school, half a semester ahead. On my last day there I got summoned to the girls' vice-principal's office and thought, "Oh, no, they're not going to tell me I can't spell and now I can't get out, are they?" but instead Mrs.

Standfast (Mrs. *Bertha* Standfast) gave me the "You are now about to embark upon the road of life" speech, which, I hoped, would keep her mind off the fact that come was dripping down my leg, hardly appropriate, but I hadn't known they didn't skip the amenities even in summer school. Usually when you have a diploma handed to you at Hollywood, it's off the stage of the Hollywood Bowl. The Hollywood Bowl seats something like 20,000 people. It must really be a smattering little ceremony with just kids and their parents there, but I suppose nobody can resist. At the time, it didn't occur to me that I'd already embarked on the road of life.

At the end of her speech she handed me a handsome black diploma case and told me my diploma would be coming in the mail since it was still at the printer's. And then she became less formal. "And what will you do now, dear?"

I'd always liked Mrs. Standfast because she had a sense of humor and she tried to keep out of people's way. (She once was tipped off that the girls were smoking in the girls' room in the Arts Bldg., and she took a delegation and the place emptied out like a clown car, and all she did was laugh and laugh, she didn't even pretend it wasn't funny. I always liked her.) So I didn't want to hurt her feelings by telling her what I planned to do. I had been one of the girls in the girls' room.

"Do?" I asked, trying to rub my calf dry.

"Yes," she said. "You have good grades but you seem to have changed your major a number of times . . . Will you go on . . . ?"

Going on meant going to UCLA, which, like Everest, was there.

"I don't know," I said. "I thought I'd go to LACC until I decided, you know?"

"Well, dear . . ." she said, not hiding her disappointment—they liked you to "go on" and not just dodge the issue by going to LACC, "Good luck."

We rose and she shook my hand.

I stuffed the diploma case into my big, open-topped purse and half fled to the girls' room, where I had a cigarette and stuffed tissue paper into my pants to be on the safe side.

Feeling more confident, I stood on the steps in front of the Administration Building, struggling in my over-crowded purse to find my sunglasses before walking up Highland to Hollywood Blvd. to take the bus, for the last time, home from school. My purse was full of its usual scandalous reading material, cigarettes, contraception and make-up as I stood beneath the hot August smoggy sun unshaded by the surrounding banana trees. Hollywood High always was unshaded by the banana trees that grew in profusion near the buildings. My sunglasses were down at the bottom next to the beer opener. I never called a beer opener a church key; the association never seemed right. I always had a beer opener with me in those days, like lipstick.

I didn't tell my flashy young man that I'd graduated from high school. He was too removed to have under-stood the American import or to have thought an empty diploma case after a speech in a room with only two peo-ple was anything to wonder about. He was a "serious" composer and had instilled in me his attitudes about things like the Four Freshmen singing "Graduation Day" and the sentimental oosh of " . . . we'll remember, always, Graduation Day" would have fallen into his scorn. I was so instilled with his world that one night I spent 15 min-utes telling a nice older man at a party that all popular music was crap and then the nice older man turned out to have written "You Make Me Feel So Young," which was my favorite song, secretly, in the whole world.

What I'll remember always was not the flashy lover, who is a watery valentine floating translucently in a half-forgotten resort of souvenirs, nor the relief of getting that diploma case. What I'll remember always was the Rainier Ale.

For the Green Death, I have reserved a kind of dazzling and cherished intensity that you hear in the voices of Frenchmen in movies when they speak of their first love, an older woman who is no more but is savored in memory to the day they die. The trouble with Rainier Ale is, it's still there. They haven't changed it, it's just a few cents more, that's all. The Frenchman can go on with his life, get married and have grandchildren—the temptation of his first love is out of reach.

Only with me, every time I go into a liquor store . . .

My flashy lover was ideal for the kind of love-comic virgin that I went as until his texture began to conflict with who I really was which had to come out sooner or later. I was not the sweet flower petal of femininity we'd conjured up for me to be when we first started and it was just as well that he got another Fulbright and was swept away to learn yet another language in the beds of yet another nation's girls. And by that time I'd begun to realize that a life of rehearsals, jam sessions, eccentric old men writing 12-tone serial pieces and being introduced to everyone as Stravinsky's goddaughter was not the life for me.

I looked like Brigitte Bardot and I was Stravinsky's goddaughter. There was nothing I could do about being named by Stravinsky and I had a feeling that no matter what I looked like, he would have had to have me just for that, for Stravinsky reasons. So I could never get too in love with him and, anyway, it was ridiculous to imagine going to concerts for much longer. I, being Stravinsky's goddaughter, spent my childhood growing up hating concerts.

But in liquor stores now when I go to the refrigerated section to pick up some of Vernor's 1 Cal (Vernor's Ginger Ale is another regional thing of beauty and unending quality, only not our region—Detroit it's from), now when I stand by the huge glass doors and search past the Cokes and Cold Duck and Squirt, sometimes as they are gliding over the rows my eyes are suddenly rooted to the emerald green-golden monarchial crests which adorn the cans of Rainier Ale. And then they boldly whisper the rapture of secret desires consummated in passion that we once stumbled upon together in the days when we never thought that such a thing as "irreconcilable differences" would have to do with us. Rainier Ale, you see, is too fattening.

Now I drink champagne.

Sins are the ones you have to give up, not the ones that don't make any difference. Champagne doesn't make any difference. Half a can of the Green Death equals five pounds. I never give up sins until the last moment, hoping that modern science will figure it out. But true sins are never ironed out either by science or art, so since all either of them could come up with was champagne, it tides me over. Sometimes, just in the first ten minutes, you get almost a hint of Rainier.

Anything that's your heart's desire, I've noticed, sooner or later turns into a sin and you're only going to wind up with hints, so you'll be lucky to get even half. Desire something enormous, the road of life being what it is. . . .

Nowadays I drink tequila when I can't get French Champagne. Graham's in London in limousines with violent beauties, though I know he'd prefer rumpled 18-year-olds just as I'd rather have Rainier. Sometimes he telephones from some studio in the middle of the night

9,000 miles away and tells me he has always loved me and
really loves me still.

"Yeah, well, send me some money," I say.

"What? I can't hear you, there's something the matter
with the phone."

He lies and I'm broke.

But when I hear that liar's chocolate voice I am, each
time, thrown into a confusion of the night he came in
alone from the stars.

My cousin Polly is graduating from high school out in
Long Island this summer. She was visiting here on New
Year's Eve and shared that can of Rainier Ale with me,
the one where I gained 5 lbs. In spite of her sophisti-
cation about drugs, I was glad to see that she got knocked
for a loop over just one glass and went dancing on Olvera
Street with the Mexicans and my parents, something far
beneath her acid dignity. She told me she hated school and
didn't know what she wanted to do and I said she could
come stay with me if I had any money by that time. She's
never seen "Zapata."

Graham said he could screen it for us when he gets back.

Mrs. Standfast would not be happy with my record. It
would not do credit to Hollywood High, whose motto is
"Seek Honor Through Service," and here I am with no
children, no dog, no husband and no divorce, even. But as
an adventuress, it is to be said that sometimes I've ridden a
white horse, clutching its mane, into blue heaven and
tasted the sins of the Green Death.

[1972]

THE OFFICE PARTY

Corey Ford

There are several methods of getting through the Christmas holidays. One is to board a ship in San Francisco and sail for the Orient, arranging to cross the International Dateline at midnight on Christmas Eve. As a result, the next day on the calendar will be December 26, and your Christmas will have been a total blank.

Another way to make your Christmas a total blank is to attend an Office Party the day before . . .

The annual Office Party starts along about noon on December 24 and ends two or three months later, depending how long it takes the boss to find out who set fire to his wastebasket, threw the water cooler out of the window, and betrayed Miss O'Malley in the men's washroom. By the time the entire Accounting Department has been dismissed and the painters have finished doing over the two lower floors which were ruined when somebody turned on the sprinkler system at the festivities' height, the moment has arrived to start planning *next* year's party, which everyone vows will be even more hilarious than the last one. *Next* year all the guests will be supplied with shin guards and hockey sticks.

Usually the merrymaking begins in a modest way, with some paper cups and a bottle of Pretty Good Stuff that Mr. Freem, in Office Supplies, received from a salesman who was anxious to land the roller-towel concession for the following year. While a few associates drop by to wish Mr. Freem a merry Yule and sample his P.G.S.,

Mr. Freem's secretary receives her annual Christmas remembrance from Mr. Freem. She accepts his gift in stony silence, owing to the fact that her employer forgot all about getting her anything until the last minute, as usual, and hastily sent her out an hour ago with five dollars and the coy instructions to buy herself something she likes but not to look at it because it's supposed to be a surprise. (Mr. Freem's secretary has settled on a particularly virulent perfume, which she knows Mr. Freem can't stand.)

Precisely at noon a sound of sleigh bells is heard, and Mr. Twitchell, the boss, emerges from his sanctum in an ill-fitting Santa Claus suit, a white beard, and a jovial smile that fools no one. Mr. Twitchell is a great believer in cementing employer-staff relationships, and as an example of co-operation between the brass and the underlings he has not only supplied refreshments for the occasion but has deducted 10 per cent from everyone's pay check to cover the cost so they'll all feel this is their party too. After a few opening remarks, in which Mr. Twitchell puts everybody in the proper holiday mood by explaining that production has slumped so badly there won't be any Christmas bonus this year, he waves his arm toward the door, and a boy from the drugstore enters with a tray of pimento-cheese sandwiches. Mr. Twitchell beams and lights a cigar, inadvertently setting fire to his false beard and thus supplying the only genuine laugh of the day.

The next hour or so is devoted to shaking hands and getting acquainted. After all, the main idea of an Office Party is for the different branches of the organization to get to know each other better, because the L. C. Twitchell Company is really just one big happy family and the sooner we all forget our restraint and get on a first-name basis with each other, the better time we'll have or Mr.

Corey Ford

Twitchell will know the reason why. The only trouble is that each branch of the organization has the private conviction that all the other branches are manned by imbeciles and crooks, and conversation between them is limited to such expressions of Yuletide cheer as "Well, you fellows in Promotion must have quite a drag, getting that new air-conditioning outfit for your floor," or "I hear a lot of heads are going to roll in Personnel the first of the year." To make matters worse, nobody is quite sure who anybody else is, and that stranger to whom you have just confided that the organization's weak link is the Front Office will presently turn out to be none other than Mr. Furbish, the first vice-president and a brother-in-law of the boss.

The only thing to do, under these circumstances, is to get good and loaded as fast as possible. After sufficient champagne has been mixed with sufficient rye, the ice is broken, and the celebrants are not only calling each other by their first names, but are adding certain endearing epithets which they have kept bottled up all year. For example, that mild, soft-spoken Mr. Murgatroyd of the Accounting Department has just backed his immediate superior into a corner and is telling him in a loud voice that he ought to know for his own good what people are saying about him, they all think he is nothing but a stuffed shirt and why doesn't he try and act like a human being for a change? (Mr. Murgatroyd will awaken in a cold sweat next morning and try to remember what he said.)

Little Miss Meeker, who isn't used to cocktails, is contributing to the general merriment by paddling barefoot in the drinking fountain. Mr. Trench of Sales, having pursued his secretary around the desks with a sprig of mistletoe, has cornered her behind the filing cabinet and is assuring her in maudlin tones that his wife doesn't

105

understand him. (As a result of these confidences, his secretary will be transferred shortly to the Chicago branch.) Mr. Phinney, the conscientious office manager, is wandering from room to room with a harried expression, retrieving the stub of a cigarette which some merrymaker has left burning on the edge of a desk, or picking up an empty highball glass and wiping off the ring of moisture from the mahogany bookcase. Mr. Phinney greets the Office Party each year with all the enthusiasm he would display toward a return attack of sciatica.

By midafternoon the party is a shambles. Paper cups, parts of sandwiches, and an occasional girdle litter the floor. Four shirt-sleeved individuals from the Traffic Department, perspiring freely, have organized a quartet and are rendering such nostalgic Christmas carols as "Jack, Jack, the Sailor Chap" and "O'Reilly's Daughter." Miss Meeker has passed out cold, with her head in a wastebasket, and the upright members of the staff are drawing lots to see which one will get her back to Staten Island. (Miss Meeker will be discovered in Van Cortlandt Park two days later, wandering around in a dazed condition.) Several fist fights have broken out in the men's room, and a first-aid station has been set up in the reception hall for the treatment of abrasions, minor contusions, and black-and-blue marks on stenographers' thighs. Mr. Twitchell remains cold sober, observing the celebrants through his pince-nez glasses and jotting down their names grimly in his little black book. Tomorrow will be Christmas, and maybe Santa Claus will leave a little pink slip in *your* stocking.

By the time the affair breaks up along toward midnight, at the request of the building superintendent and a squadron of police, so much ill will has been generated among the staff that it will take at least twelve months for the organization to get back to normal, and then it will be time for next year's Office Party.

The only solution I know is to stage an Office Party of your own on December 23, two days before Christmas. If you get sufficiently fried, you may wander by mistake into the wrong Office Party the following noon. Not only will the proceedings be about the same as the party in your own office, but you won't get fired.

And a Merry Christmas to you, courtesy of the L. C. Twitchell Company.

[1950]

STILL LIFE WITH WOODPECKER

Tom Robbins

The temples, the minarets, the oasis, the pyramids, the camel itself filtered through her vision without being seen. Her orbs, as if conditioned by years of literacy, settled on the message that federal law required the manufacturer to publish on the left side panel of the package.

> *Warning: The Surgeon General Has Determined That Cigarette Smoking is Dangerous to Your Health.*

. . . typeface, blue ink, background as white as the eye skin around her blue irises, as white as the library rug used to be.

In her mind, clumps of tumors bloomed; soft pink lungs took on the appearance of charred firewood; grotesque tubers, oozing blood and spore jelly, spread like mushrooms across an unsuspecting lawn; arteries withered like the tendrils of parched orchids; clots resembling rotten tomatoes or the brains of diseased monkeys choked the organism, each clot emitting faint wisps of smoke from a combustion that would not die until the organism died.

Leigh-Cheri grunted in disgust. "Yuk," she said aloud, exercising the alternate mantra. "Bernard claims that a cigarette is a friend when you're locked away. With friends like these, who needs enemies?"

To the Princess, it was an enigma why anyone would smoke, yet the answer seems simple enough when we station ourselves at that profound interface of nature and culture formed when people take something from the natural world and incorporate it into their bodies.

Three of the four elements are shared by all creatures, but fire was a gift to humans alone. Smoking cigarettes is as intimate as we can become with fire without immediate excruciation. Every smoker is an embodiment of Prometheus, stealing fire from the gods and bringing it on back home. We smoke to capture the power of the sun, to pacify Hell, to identify with the primordial spark, to feed on the marrow of the volcano. It's not the tobacco we're after but the fire. When we smoke, we are performing a version of the fire dance, a ritual as ancient as lightning.

Does that mean that chain smokers are religious fanatics? You must admit there's a similarity.

The lung of the smoker is a naked virgin thrown as a sacrifice into the godfire.

Having nothing else to read, Leigh-Cheri eventually read the rest of the package. *Camel: Turkish & Domestic Blend Cigarettes: Choice: Quality: Manufactured by R.J. Reynolds Tobacco Co., Winston-Salem, N.C. 27102, U.S.A.; 20 Class A Cigarettes;* and the famous inscription that has graced the rear panel of the package since its creation in 1913 (the year, allegedly, of the last Argonian transmission to redheaded earthlings); *Don't look for premiums or coupons, as the cost of the tobaccos blended in Camel Cigarettes prohibits the use of them.*

She tried to count the *e*'s in that sentence, running into the same difficulty that has plagued many another package reader: almost nobody counts them accurately the first time. Staring at the camel, she detected a woman and a lion hidden in its body. On tiptoes, she held the pack before the one clear windowpane and saw in its reflection that the word CHOICE reads the same in its mirror image as it does on the pack, it is not turned around by the mirror. That might have tipped her off that the Camel package crosses dimensional boundaries, the line between matter and antimatter, but she failed to grasp its significance right away. It was just another parlor game. As when she searched for additional camels on the package. (There are two behind the pyramid.)

Leigh-Cheri wondered if Bernard read his Camel pack also. She decided that he must, and she felt all the closer to him, just as daily Bible readings maintained a bond between knights and ladies separated during the Crusades.

Upon rising in the morning and before retiring at night, the Princess read the Camel pack. Sometimes she read it during the day. The words were soothing to her. They were simple and straightforward. They did not set her mind to whizzing, as could the literature on certain other packages. Cheerios, for example.

On the right side-panel of the verbose and somewhat tautological box of Cheerios, it is written,

If you are not satisfied with the quality and/or performance of the Cheerios in this box, send name, address, and reason for dissatisfaction—along with *entire* boxtop and price paid—to: General Mills, Inc. Box 200-A, Minneapolis, Minn., 55460. Your purchase price will be returned.

It isn't enough that there is a defensive tone to those words, a slant of doubt, an unappetizing broach of the subject of money, but they leave the reader puzzling over exactly what might be meant by the "performance" of the Cheerios.

Could the Cheerios be in bad voice? Might not they handle well on curves? Do they ejaculate too quickly? Has

110

age affected their timing or are they merely in a mid-season slump? Afflicted with nervous exhaustion or broken hearts, are the Cheerios smiling bravely, insisting that the show must go on?

One thing you can say for the inscription, it makes you want to rush to the pantry, seize a box of Cheerios, rip back its tab (being careful not to tear it off lest there come a time to send in the boxtop, which must be *entire*), part the waxed paper inner bag with both hands, dispatch a significant minority of the Cheerio population head over heels into a bowl, douse them immediately with a quantity of milk (presumedly, they do not perform when dry), sprinkle some white sugar on top, and then, crouch, face close to the bowl, watching, evaluating, as the tiny, tan, lightweight oat doughnuts, irregular in size, tone, and texture, begin to soak up the milk and the sugar granules dissolved therein, growing soft and soggy, expanding somewhat as liquid is absorbed; and you may be thinking all the while about the toroid shape, the shape of the cyclone, the vortex, the whirlpool, the shape of a thing made of itself yet mysteriously distinct from itself; thinking about rings, halos, men overboard, the unbroken cycle of life, the void as nucleus, or, best of all, bodily orifices; thinking about whatever the trove of toroidal trinkets might inspire as, center holes flooded with sugary milk, they relax and go blobby in the bowl; but appraising, even as your mind wanders, appraising, testing, criticizing, asking repeatedly; do Cheerios measure up to Wheaties with beer, would they mix well with batshit in times of strife, would Ed Sullivan have signed them, would Knute Rockne have recruited them, how well do these little motherfuckers *perform?*

At times such as these, you understand what the man meant when he said he'd walk a mile for a Camel.

•

Leigh-Cheri began to reckon time in terms of Gulietta. When Gulietta brought lunch, it was noon. When Gulietta brought dinner, it was six in the evening. When Gulietta emptied the chamber pot, it was either 8:00 A.M. or 8:00 P.M.—for whatever the difference was worth. When Gulietta fetched her to the third-floor bath (seldom used by Max or Tilli) for a scrubbing, the Princess knew that it was Saturday and another week had passed. After ninety baths, ninety soapings of the peachfish, her lover would be eligible for parole. Gulietta was her clock and her calendar. Time was a skinny old woman with dilated pupils.

As for space, it came to be less defined by the walls of the attic, more defined by the Camel pack. The Camel pack was a rectangular solid, two and three-quarters inches high, two and one-eighth inches wide and three-quarters of an inch deep. Imagine Leigh-Cheri's eyes crawling over every crinkle in the cellophane. Imagine Leigh-Cheri gazing expectantly, her eyes like a couple of goldfish with insufficient water in their bowls.

As an environmentalist, she might have been more interested in the chamber pot. Not only did the pot have a benevolent, ecologically sound function, but its round shape—as biomorphic as a breast, melon, or moon— evoked the natural world. Yet it was the Camel pack, all right angles and parallel lines (the formal equivalent of the rational mind); it was the Camel pack, born on the drawing board far from the bulrushes; it was the Camel pack, of a shape designed to shield us from the capricious, which is to say, the inexplicable; it was the logically, synthetically geometric Camel pack that enlivened the air of her cell.

In the morning, about a quarter till Gulietta-empty-chamber-pot, Leigh-Cheri would wake to find the Camel pack beside her cot. It had the poise of an animal. Some mornings, it would be lying on the foam rubber beside her unpillowed head, like a jewel forced out of her ear by a dream. Once, or maybe twice, lying there of a morning, she placed the pack mischievously in the nest of her pubis. What strange bird laid this egg?

She spent a lot of time tossing the Camel pack in the air and catching it. She became skilled to the point where she could catch it behind her back, over her shoulder, in her teeth, or with her eyes closed. Prancing with it, she incorporated it into some old cheerleader routines. Mostly, though, she just sat holding it, staring into its exotic vistas, populating its landscape, colonizing it, learning to survive there.

When crossing the desert, she learned to swaddle herself in a burnoose, the way the natives did. Redheads burn easily. She learned which stones one could squeeze water from. She learned to appreciate the special reality of the mirage.

One day she believed that she heard the rat-a-tat of a woodpecker, but search as she might, she could find no bill holes in the trunks of the palms.

Whether on foot or camelback, Leigh-Cheri went about with eyes downcast. Leigh-Cheri was looking for matchsticks. She looked for the print of black boots in the sand.

Baths went by. Meals passed. Deposits were made in the chamber pot and subsequently withdrawn. The springtime turned slowly to summer. By the end of June, it was so stuffy in the attic it was difficult to breathe—but there was always a cool breeze at the oasis.

Leigh-Cheri would sit in the shade by the spring, playing toss-and-catch with her package of Camels. For hours on end, she would toss and catch, toss and catch, while from the spring waters big old green amphibians spied on her with that voyeuristic bulbousness that can trap beauty and fix a thing forever. She was reminded of A'ben Fizel, the look he had when he was courting her.

Periodically, nomads came to the spring. They, men as well as women, wore hand-hammered silver jewelry that jangled like cash registers in a shopkeeper's dream of heaven. Their antique rifles were as long as fishing poles, and the clay jugs that they filled with water were made black when Jesus was just a gleam in the One Big Eye. Berbers came, and Bedouins, driving their dromedaries to drink. Sheiks came, sheiks without oil wells or sons at Oxford, but who nevertheless wore robes that would pump up the egos of every silkworm in the East, and who vanished in clouds of perfume so thick they made the Princess cough.

Invariably, she questioned those traders, raiders, belly dancers, ali babas, and caravan executives about any red-haired outlaws they might have passed on their route, while they in turn hit her up for cigarettes.

"But I can't open the pack," she'd try to explain. "If I did, all this would collapse. A successful external reality depends upon an internal vision that is left intact."

They glared at her the way any intelligent persons ought to glare when what they need is a smoke, a bite, a cup of coffee, a piece of ass, or a good fast-paced story, and all they're getting is philosophy.

[1980]

HENRY AND JUNE

Anaïs Nin

Hugo and I are in the car, driving to an elegant evening. I sing until it seems my singing is driving the car. I swell my chest and imitate the *roucoulement* of the pigeons. My French *rrrrrrrrrr* roll. Hugo laughs. Later, with a marquis and a marquise, we come out of the theatre, and whores press in around us, very close. The marquise tightens her mouth. I think, they are Henry's whores, and I feel warmly towards them, friendly.

One evening I suggest to Hugo that we go to an "exhibition" together, just to see. "Do you want to?" I say, although in my mind I am ready to live, not to see. He is curious, elated. "Yes, yes." We call up Henry to ask for information. He suggests 32 rue Blondel.

On the way over, Hugo hesitates, but I am laughing at his side, and I urge him on. The taxi drops us in a narrow little street. We had forgotten the number. But I see "32" in red over one of the doorways. I feel that we have stood on a diving board and have plunged. And now we are in a play. We are different.

I push a swinging door. I was to go ahead to barter over the price. But when I see it is not a house but a café full of people and naked women, I come back to call Hugo, and we walk in.

Noise. Blinding lights. Many women surrounding us, calling us, trying to attract our attention. The *patronne* leads us to a table. Still the women are shouting and signaling. We must choose. Hugo smiles, bewildered.

I glance over them. I choose a very vivid, fat, coarse Spanish-looking woman, and then I turn away from the shouting group to the end of the line and call a woman who had made no effort to attract my attention, small, feminine, almost timid. Now they sit before us.

The small woman is sweet and pliant. We talk, oh, so politely. We discuss each other's nails. They comment on the unusualness of my nacreous nail polish. I ask Hugo to look carefully to see if I have chosen well. He does and says I could not have done better. We watch the women dancing. I see only in spots, intensely. Certain places are utter blanks to me. I see big hips, buttocks, and sagging breasts, so many bodies, all at once. We had expected there would be a man for the exhibition. "No," says the *patronne*, "but the two girls will amuse you. You will see everything." It would not be Hugo's night, then, but he accepts everything. We barter over the price. The women smile. They assume it is my evening because I have asked them if they will show me lesbian poses.

Everything is strange to me and familiar to them. I only feel at ease because they are people who need things, whom one can do things for. I give away all my cigarettes. I wish I had a hundred packets. I wish I had a lot of money. We are going upstairs. I enjoy looking at the women's naked walk.

The room is softly lighted and the bed low and ample. The women are cheerful, and they wash themselves. How the taste for things must wear down with so much automatism. We watch the big woman tie a penis on herself, a rosy thing, a caricature. And they take poses, nonchalantly, professionally. Arabian, Spanish, Parisienne, love when one does not have the price of a hotel room, love in a taxi, love when one of the partners is sleepy . . .

Hugo and I look on, laughing a little at their sallies. We learn nothing new. It is all unreal, until I ask for the lesbian poses.

The little woman loves it, loves it better than the man's approach. The big woman reveals to me a secret place in the woman's body, a source of a new joy, which I had sometimes sensed but never definitely—that small core at the opening of the woman's lips, just what the man passes by. There, the big woman works with the flicking of her tongue. The little woman closes her eyes, moans, and trembles in ecstasy. Hugo and I lean over them, taken by that moment of loveliness in the little woman, who offers to our eyes her conquered, quivering body. Hugo is in turmoil. I am no longer woman; I am man. I am touching the core of June's being.

I become aware of Hugo's feelings and say, "Do you want the woman? Take her. I swear to you I won't mind, darling."

"I could come with anybody just now," he answers.

The little woman is lying still. Then they are up and joking and the moment passes. Do I want . . . ? They unfasten my jacket; I say no, I don't want anything.

I couldn't have touched them. Only a minute of beauty —the small woman's heaving, her hands caressing the other woman's head. That moment alone stirred my blood with another desire. If we had been a little madder . . . But the room seemed dirty to us. We walked out. Dizzy. Joyous. Elated.

We went to dance at the Bal Nègre. One fear was over. Hugo was liberated. We had understood each other's feelings. Together. Arm in arm. A mutual generosity.

I was not jealous of the little woman Hugo had desired. But Hugo thought, "What if there had been a man . . . " So we don't know yet. All we know is that the evening was beautifully carried off. I had been able to give Hugo a portion of the joy that filled me.

And when we returned home, he adored my body because it was lovelier than what he had seen and we sank into sensuality together with new realization. We are killing phantoms.

[1931]

THE GINGER MAN

J. P. Donleavy

Raining outside. Cold morning. Felicity in her pram in the kitchen, wiggling a toothbrush in a jam jar. Marion standing against the mantelpiece in front of the black empty grate. Wearing slippers, wrapped in a blanket, her shanks showing. Just finished reading the letter, folding it carefully and slipping it back into its envelope.

I could tell there was trouble. I came down the stairs with my usual innocence and pain right smack into her silence which is the sign that she has a weapon. She stood there as if she were watching the groom saddle her horse. There was a smear of lipstick at the corner of her mouth, gave her a twisted smile. I thought for a second she was an Inca. She was quite polite when I asked her who the letter was from. She said simply, from your father.

"I'll get my glasses."

"I'm afraid the letter is addressed to me."

"What do you mean, you're afraid?"

"Just that. You're not going to read it."

"Now just a minute, that letter is from my father and I intend to know what's in it."

"And I intend you shan't."

"Don't get snotty."

"I'll be as snotty as I want. I no longer have to tolerate your nastiness."

"What's this mumbo jumbo. Don't act as if you have a secret file on me."

"I assure you it's not mumbo jumbo. I'm leaving this house."

"Now look, Marion, I don't feel well. I'm not up to farting about at this godforsaken hour of the morning. Now just what the hell do you mean you're leaving this house?"

"Leaving this house."

"There's a lease."

"I know there's a lease."

"For three years."

"I know it's for three years."

Marion's eyebrows raised. She kept reaching over her shoulder, pulling the blanket up. Sebastian stood in the doorway wearing a pair of purple pajamas, bright red slippers and a gray turtle necked sweater, its yarn unravelling, the string suspended behind him and disappearing up the stairs.

"Ah for Jesus sake, now let's not get started. I only want to know what you're talking about. You know, just for the sake of making things clear, I'll never get this damned exam if I have to face more misunderstanding. Now what is it? Has my father made you an offer of money or something?"

"You're not reading the letter."

"All right. I'm not reading the letter. Now tell me, what the hell is this all about?"

"Your father is on my side."

"Look Marion, all right. Now we know that you have everything your way. I know the drivel in that letter. Probably sent you a check."

"As a matter of fact, he did."

"Told you that I've always been a bastard."

"Quite."

"Expelled from schools."

"Yes."

"All right. What are you going to do?"

"Move from here, instantly."

"Where?"

"I'm going to see an agent this morning."

"What about the lease?"

"That's your doing."

"You stupid bitch."

"Go right ahead. Say anything you want. It matters nothing to me. By the way, you've left half my sweater on the stairs."

"Now, Marion, let's understand each other. I don't feel that this fighting is going to get us anywhere."

"It's certainly not going to get you anywhere."

"Now look, how much is the check."

"That's my business."

"I've got to get my typewriter out of the pawn. I must have it for my notes."

"Ha. Ha. Ha."

Marion's mocking head back, disdainfully shutting eyes. The blue vein, handsome and large on the blonde throat. Pink slip and her shanks shifting the slippers, grinding the coal dust on the floor.

"Supposing I admit to a few indiscretions."

"Indiscretions? That really is amusing you know."

"Now that we have a chance to start over again."

"We do, do we? O we. It's we now."

"I'm thinking about the lease."

"You signed it."

Sebastian turned and went quietly up the stairs. Tip toe, tip toe. Dragging the wool string behind. Into the bedroom. Dropping the purples, pulling on the trousers. Tied a knot in the sweater. Put his sockless feet into shoes. A jacket for the respect that was in it. And my dear pair of golfing shoes. Pity, but must to the pawn. Ten and six for sure. Now my dear Marion, I'll give you a little something to think about.

In the toilet, Sebastian forced a board up from the floor. He hammered a nail through the lead pipe with the heel of his golfing shoe. He went quickly down the stairs. Marion saw him pass out the hall. The door squeaked shut.

I'll say one thing. She's not going to pull this stuff much longer. This is final. If she wants it this way, this way it shall be.

In this bitterness and hazy hatred. No cozy road to the swelled udders. This is at the midnight of everything. Because when I was living in America I had a lot of good things. I never had to think about hot water. I went to my club where it was running rampant. Stand under a shower and let it beat the head. Soothed me. Ease and comfort and quiet is all I want. And on this damn tram I'm riding into the face of debt and other things as well. I'm a college student standing on the chapel steps with the white paper which says I know the law of Contract and can be paid starvation wages for a year. My certificate that I won't steal from the open till but I'm a gentleman and I'll close the till after rifling it.

Four o'clock on this oblong Tuesday. Sebastian pushing through the door of a secret public house, moved cautiously to an empty space at the bar. Bartender suspiciously approaching him.

"I want a triple Irish, Gold Label. Quickly please."

"Sir, I'm afraid I can't serve you."

"You what?"

"Can't serve you, sir, rules of the house, you've had enough to drink."

"I've had enough to drink? What on earth do you mean?"

"I think, sir, you've had sufficient unto your needs now. I think you've had enough now."

"This is contemptible."

"Peacefully sir, now. Keep the peace. When you're sober sir, now, be very glad to serve you. Little sleep. You'll be fine."

"Frightful outrage. Are you sure you're not drunk yourself?"

"Now sir, a place and time for everything."

"Well for Jesus sake."

Sebastian turned from the bar pushed out through the door and along the street. In dazed condition. Along the pavement by shop windows with pens and pencils and stone steps to Georgian doors and black spokes of fences and by a tea shop with gray women clustered at the tables. So I'm drunk. Strangled Christ. Drunk. Nothing to do but suffer this insult as I have suffered so many others. It will die away in a few years, no worry about that. I'm going on a tram ride. Dalkey. That nice little town out there on the rocks with pretty castles and everything. A place where I will move when the quids are upon me. I hate this country. I think I hate this country more than anything else I know. Drunk. That son of a bitch, take him up by the ears from behind the bar and beat him against the ceiling. But must forget the whole thing. I'm at the bottom of the pile. Admit that I'm in such a state that I can barely think. But I won't be insulted. Incredible outrage.

He passed in front of the Kildare Street Club, crossed over the street and waited for the tram, leaning against the railings of Trinity College.

Isn't that a beautiful place. In spite of all rejections and refusals. But I remember a pitiful time in there, too. During the first week in the dining hall. Autumn's October and I was so very chilly that year because the weather was bad. But it was nice to get in there because there is a thick pipe that goes all around the walls and it is filled with hot water. And it's such a big room, with enormous portraits high up on the wall which kept me well in the center in case one fell on my head. But it is such a very pleasant experience to go into this dining hall on a Dublin cold day and say, how do, to the lovely woman at the door taking gowns and move along in the academic line with a tin tray. On magic days with half crown, it is so delicious to take a Chelsea bun and a little white dish. Further along the line on the top tables there are nice little balls of butter. All balls are bells. Then there is the woman with the white hair who serves out the potatoes. How are you now? And on these days with that ever ready half crown I'd get a rabbit pie from the delightful lady with the red hair who got younger every day and then say, ever so quietly, because these were magic words—and some sprouts too, please. Not the last. No. Further along the line. Trays covered with trifle. Had to get there early to get the trifle because it was so good that it was gone fast. Next table, a jug of sugar because I was going to get some cream to put on a banana, all slices and mixed in the cup and then at last to the cash desk. My tragic two and six. And this day I was so very hungry. I went through the line gathering all the food, arranging it with care. And my head was hard and thick from thinking and tired eyes. My tray skidded from my fingers and fell on the floor. My orange jelly mixed with broken glass on this day when I bought a glass of milk to have with my Chelsea bun. They told me I was clumsy and asked why did I do it. And at times in my heart there is a music that plays for me. Tuneless threnody. They called me names. I was so afraid of them. And they could never look inside me and see a whole world of tenderness or leave me alone because I was so sad and suffering. Why did you do it. And hearts. And why was love so round.

Tram swaying down the flat street. Squealing and stopping. Sitting all the way and dreaming. Even passing 1 Mohammed. Perhaps I was a bastard to lay foul the pipes again. Make her know she needs me. And I need that money. Out in Dalkey I'll be all alone. No fear of meeting anyone.

He arrived in the main street. Twisted with people. Into a public house. Two lovely, laughing girls behind the bar.

"Good day, sir."

"Double Gold Label, please."

She reached under the bar. Always hiding the stuff. Damn girl with her gold, cheap bracelets, earrings, damn pair of gold tits, squirting out money.

"And twenty Woodbines."

Under the bar again. Out with them smiling and wagging her eyes. Rows of bottles of wine and minerals and port and sherry there for years. As decorations for drinking stout. A lot of rich people live out here in Dalkey. Big houses on the sea. I like it. And take a walk along the Vico Road and see across Killiney Bay to Bray. A change of scene is good for a change of mind. And the mortification of being treated like a drunkard is dreadful for me as stark and stone sober as I am.

"I wonder could I have a pint of porter, please."

"Certainly, sir."

Lot of work pumping that out. I like this pretty girl. I have a passion for her. I know I have passion. Through that window the yellow sun is coming in. Those men down there are talking about me. I don't get along with men.

"And another small one."

"Gold Label?"

"Please."

I was a curious little boy. Sent to the proper places. And went to most improper ones. Secret and sinful and I even worked once. I think it is quite a common thing, start at the bottom. He, ha, haw, eke. But when you have so many problems it's not easy to be distracted into the past. I was a spoiled child I should suppose. Quickly given to lies. And gross falsehoods to teachers, mostly out of fear I guess. But what would I have done without the odd lie these days. I remember a teacher telling me I pouted and was ugly. Which wasn't true. I was an extremely handsome, curious child. Teachers are insensitive to true beauty.

"What's your name?"

"Gertrude."

"May I call you Gertrude?"

"Yes."

"Gertrude, will you give me another Gold Label and a pint of porter?"

"Yes."

I went to a proper preparatory school, preparing for college. I never felt that these schools were good enough for me. I was aloof. Never seeking friends. But my silence was noticed by the teachers and they thought that I was a shifty article and once I heard them telling very rich boys to stay away from me because I wasn't a good influence. Then I got older and bolder. A wanton girl who had pock marks on her face and stubs of hair all up her legs when I thought girls' legs were always nice and smooth, took me into the city from the suburbs where I lived and we drank in bars. When she felt all pally and possessive and sensing my reserve and fright she said that I ought not to wear a striped tie with a striped shirt and I kept saying to myself, hiding the hurt, that I just put on the shirt quickly and the tie in a rush. And when we went home together on the subway train she slept with her head on my shoulder. I felt

embarrassed because she looked old and tough. A girl who
ran away, was expelled from schools and smoked when she
was twelve. And me, I was always somehow getting to
know these girls, not out of sex or sin, but because their
souls were fetched up out of them by dismal sodas and
dances and they would see me with my big, shrewdless
eyes and come and invite me to sneak a cigarette or drink.

"Gertrude, you're very good behind the bar. I want a
really big lash of Gold Label."

Gertrude smiled at Kathleen.

I was nineteen and older and in a sailor suit and back in
Virginia and Norfolk. On leave I would go to the libraries
because in behind the stacks I could escape. Sunny days
meant nothing to me. And I made a trip to Baltimore.
Into a strange boarding house on a dry cold New Year's
Eve. The wind blowing. My room had no windows. Just
an open transom. All the time I was in that part of
America I felt the closeness of the Great Dismal Swamp
and broken boards and peeling signs and road houses
isolated with greed and silence, drink and snakes. I walked
about the city, lost and trying to get it. Put it in one spot
and look at it and stand there with all Baltimore around
me where I could pick it up in my hand and take it away.
But move on and up and down and around each street and
find it blank and unimportant without the rest. I went into
a bar, crowded and dark, tripping over people's legs.
Voices, sighs and laughs and lies and lips and teeth and
whites of eyes. Secrets of shaved armpits and the thin,
small hair on women's upper lips showing through tan
powders. All these breasts slung in rayon cradles. I pushed
through elbows to the bar and sat on a red and chromium
stool. Sitting beside me, a girl in a black, ungainly dress.
Down on her leg I saw net stockings. Curious girl with
large brown eyes in her round face of rough skin and thin

lips. Here in Baltimore. Sitting, searching at a bar. There was a dreadful fight. And the abuse. Cheapskate, tough and wise. And bastard. There are babes present, buddy. I'd like to see you do it, who's pushing who, come outside, say, watch your language, no cheap son of a bitch, hit him for Christ's sake, hit him. In the middle of all this tiresome behavior she turned to me and said hello, smiled slightly, weakly and said you look so much more peaceful. I asked her to have a drink and she said yes, but she didn't need a dozen drinks to have a good time, or drink all evening because I'm here because I wanted to do something different, and really, you don't mind me picking you up. Her black hair combed straight down around her head and I listened to her talking in her rich, pleasant and kindly voice. I just walked in here alone and now I'm talking to a sailor—yes, I'd like to share a bottle of champagne with you, I would like it—I've never had it before—is it nice? And why did you come in here? I hope you'll forgive my conduct, but I'm just curious. She was a girl who was soft and clean. And she said I am being presumptuous and forward. I don't intend to be—I'm just a little groggy, I bought myself three whiskies. I've been promising myself to just someday walk into a bar by myself and sit up and drink with other people, but it took New Year's Eve to make me do it—no one is being themselves on New Year's are they? Or don't you care? I told her she was very likeable. And saw her eyes light. Is that why you're buying a bottle of champagne, because I'm likeable? I hope you are. I feel rather good—giggly and silly and you're quiet and reserved, aren't you? And I'm just sitting here talking to you, an utter stranger and just going on and on—well I'll tell you about me. I'm at college and I don't really like it because I don't have any time to enjoy it because I have to work and I don't get dated, never been to a nightclub—

I'm curious, naturally, but it's contrary to everything I
believe, I mean the frivolous, sophisticated life of society
people. I don't hold that sort of thing important—and
I'll tell you the truth—that really I came in here because
I didn't have a date on this night of nights and I told
myself that anyway I would buy myself a drink and if
anyone talked to me I would talk to them but I talked to
you first because you looked as if I could talk to you and
you would be nice and you're alone too, aren't you? And
I'm not a brave girl so much as a frustrated one. I've just
walked into a bar, and I was frightened to death that
the barman would tell me that women without escorts
couldn't come in. Now that I'm here it all seemed so very
simple and easy and I'm glad I did. And I'm beginning to
see that that is the way to do a lot of things in life—just to
go ahead and do them. I saw you coming in and I just
thought to myself that you looked rather nice and then
you were next to me and I just felt like talking to you—so
I did—and now where are we? She told me she had only
one request to make—that she didn't want me to know
her name because she might regret everything, and not
to spend so much money on her, a stranger, that they
would probably never see each other again, anyway. She
was warm. I pressed my nose through her straight black
hair and my lips behind her ear, whispering I liked her
and please stay with me. She put her face in front of mine
and said distinctly, if that means you want to go to bed
with me or if you want me to come to bed with you, I'll
be blunt, I will. Whole hearted. Blunt. And I'm not trying
to be whorish. But I suppose I am. Am I? Or what. What
do you expect of a girl like me? And I don't suppose after
that remark you would believe I don't have any idea of
how to go to bed with a man. But where and how and
when? There's a whole lot to it, isn't there?

Sebastian stood up, taking his glass to this bar in Dalkey, waiting behind the figures.

"A double Gold Label."

Returning to his seat. Sitting slowly and putting out his legs, crossing his knees, shaking his foot and placing his glass within the circle movement of his arm. The public house was filling with the seven o'clock after work after dinner faces.

I brought her to a room in a large, prominent hotel in Baltimore and we passed by the mobbed streets and a girl dancing on top of a taxi, sailors and soldiers clutching at her ankles. Pulling at her clothes until they were ripping them from her body. Hands taking her apart. In the room she said she was a little frightened. We had more champagne. On one twin bed I sat down, excited. I talked to her. Twister that I was. Heart of hoax. Bluffing my way into her hands. Carrying her down beside me. Heard her in my ear. I'm frightened. I'm scared. Don't force me to do anything, will you? But I think you're kind. And I'm just a little blasé and not caring, but I worry very much what's going to happen to me, really. But after a while you get to hate everyone and everybody and you get very bitter inside because you haven't money and clothes and wealthy boyfriends asking you out to smart places and even though you know that really all of it is false, it somehow manages to seep in and you find yourself resenting the fact that all you have is a good brain and you're smarter than they are but would like to wear false breasts because your own are flat but you feel it's such a horrid lie and yet they do it and get away with it and then in the end you're faced with the blunt truth that they will get married and you won't and that they are going to hate their marriages but then they will have tea parties and cocktails and bridge while their husbands are sleeping with other men. She was a girl gone away. And I put my finger in her sad, tight, little hole, feeling lost and crying and wandering in rain and trees, a world too big, and lost and her dark head was so dark and her eyes shut.

He brought his glass back to the bar, and walked out. Get on the tram. On to the tram because we are all going to East Geenga. I'm a man for getting off at the end of the line. I've had more than I can bear. Take me on the ship, away. To Florida. I drove my big car right through The Everglades. A little wet and soggy. I used to walk around Fort Lauderdale drunk and diving in the canals at night killing alligators. And drive along Miami Beach steering with my toes. What do you want me to do. Stay on this dreary stage of churchbound hopelessness? This country is foreign to me. I want to go back to Baltimore. I've never had a chance to see everything, or ride the trains, or see all the little towns. Pick up girls in amusement parks. Or smell them with the peanuts in Suffolk, Virginia. I want to go back.

Quick feet up the street. Seeing nothing on either side. No houses or stairs or iron spokes of fences. Half running, tripping, pounding, pulling the air aside.

Slow down. Nonchalant, and careful too, while going in, possessed with reserve and other things as well and we will see about this.

The bar was filled with old men. Spitting secrets in each other's ears. Smoke coming over the top of all the snugs. Faces turning as Dangerfield comes in. The sound of corks ripped pop. Ends of bottles bang on the bar. Seaweedy foam rising in the wet glasses. Rudeness must be dealt with. Swiftly. Put them down, I say, not up, down and don't spare the clubs.

Sebastian stepped to the bar, stood dignified and quiet. Bartender removing bottles. Comes along up to him. His eyes meeting the red ones and he nods his head to this tall customer.

"Yes?"

"A double Gold Label."

Bartender turns a few steps and back with the bottle, tense and pouring.

"Water?"

"Soda."

Bartender goes, gets the soda bottle. Squirt, squirt. A blast coming out of it. Whoops. The whiskey shot up the sides of the glass, splashing on the bar.

"Sorry, sir."

"Yes."

"It's a new bottle."

"Quite."

Bartender puts away the bottle and comes back for the money. Stands embarrassed in front of Dangerfield. Licking his lips, ready to speak, but waits, says nothing. Dangerfield looking at him. The old men sensing disaster, turning on their stools to watch.

"Two shillings."

"I was in this public house this afternoon about four o'clock. Do you remember?"

"I do."

"And you refused to serve me."

"Yes."

"On the grounds that I was drunk. Is that correct?"

"That's correct."

"Do you think I am drunk now?"

"That's not for me to decide."

"You decided that this afternoon. I repeat. Do you think I am drunk now?"

"I want no trouble."

"Half my whiskey is on the bar."

"No trouble now."

"Would you mind bringing me the bottle to replace the amount splashed in my face."

Bartender in his white shirt and sleeves rolled up brings back the bottle. Sebastian taking out the cork and filling his glass to the brim.

"You can't do that. We don't have much of that."

"I repeat. Do you think I'm drunk now."

"Now peacefully, no trouble, no trouble, we don't want any trouble here. No, I don't think you're drunk. Not drunk. Little excited. No."

"I'm a sensitive person. I hate abuse. Let them all hear."

"Quietly now, peace."

"Shut up while I'm talking."

All the figures spinning about on their stools and flat feet.

"No trouble now, no trouble."

"Shut up. Am I drunk? Am I drunk?"

"No."

"Why you Celtic lout. I am. I'm drunk. Hear me, I'm drunk and I'm going to level this kip, level it to the ground, and anyone who doesn't want his neck broken get out."

The whiskey bottle whistled past the bartender's head, splattering in a mass of glass and gin. Dangerfield drank off the whiskey in a gulp and a man up behind him with a stout bottle which he broke on Dangerfield's head, stout dripping over his ears and down his face, reflectively licking it from around his mouth. The man in horror ran from the building. The bartender went down the trap door in the floor. Sebastian over the bar standing on it. Selecting a bottle of brandy for further reference. Three brave figures at the door peering in upon the chaos and saying stop him, as this Danger made for the door and one man's hand reached out to grab him and it was quickly twisted till the fingers broke with his squeal of agony and the other two lay back to attack from behind and he jumped phoof on Dangerfield's shoulders and was flipped neatly on his arse five paces down the street. The rest had gone to doorways or posing that they were just out walking their dogs.

Dangerfield was running like a madman down the middle of the road with the cry get the guards pushing him faster. Into a laneway, bottle stuffed under his arm. More yells as they caught sight as he went round and down another street. Must for the love of God get hidden. Up these steps and got to get through this door somehow and out of sight quick.

Heart pounding, leaning on the wall for breath. A bicycle against the wall. Dark and racy for sure. Hope. Wait till they are by the house. Feet. I hear the heavy heels of a peeler. Pray for me. If they get me I'll be disgraced. Must avoid capture for the sake of the undesirable publicity it will produce. Or they may take clubs to me. Suffering shit.

The door opens slowly. Light shining in through the dark. Dangerfield moves cautiously behind the door as it widens against him. A small head peers in, hesitates. I must be upon him for the sake of safety. Sebastian drove his shoulder against the door pulling the figure in by the neck.

"If you so much as breathe I'll belt you to death."

"No. Jesus, Mary and Joseph I won't make a peep."

"Shut up. Give me that hat. And the coat."

"O none of that, I'm a man of God. You don't know where to stop."

"I'll stop you living if you don't shut up and give me that coat."

"Yes sir. Anything you want sir, anything, but don't

harm an old man, sir. I'm a cripple from birth, sir and I'll help ye get away. All I can."

"Get up the stairs."

"What are ye going to do with me at all. I've got a Friday to go out of the nine first Fridays."

"You won't have a minute to go if you don't get up the stairs. Up to the top and stay there. If you utter a sound I'll come back and disembowel you."

The little blue-eyed man stepped backwards up the stairs, stopping at the first landing and ran tripping up the rest. Sebastian getting into the coat. Shoulders get in, sleeves at the elbows. He bends over to pick up the brandy. The coat parts down the back. Peers out the door. No one in sight. Take all care, proceed with caution. How did I ever get into this frightful mess. How fantastically undesirable.

Down the three granite steps. Which way? From around the corner, a blue uniform and helmet. God's unmerciful teeth. The Guard stops, looks, starts forward up the street. Dangerfield setting his vehicle firmly in the gutter, straddling it, pushes off pumping fearfully followed by the voice of the little man out the top window of the building.

"That's him all right. He's got me coat and hat. That's him."

The bike moves off speedily up the narrow road and around the corner into a screaming of horns and the bottle slides, bangs his knee and breaks with a wet pop on the street. Policeman in the middle of the road directing traffic. Putting his hand up to stop. Couldn't know it was me. Can't take the chance, onward you crazy christian soldier, peddling off to doom.

"Hey you, stop there. Stop there you. You hear me, stop. Hey."

Helter skelter for St. Stephen's Green. Bike wiggling on the cobbles, skidding on the tram tracks. Dangerfield bent double over the handlebars. Licking his lips. Eyes wet with the wind, blinking and blind. They'll have the patrol car, if they have one, after me or maybe motor bikes or the whole force on roller skates. Traffic lights ahead. Whoa. Red for stop.

The bike making a wide arc in front of the oncoming traffic. More horns and screech of brakes. And on down the street aswarm with children until one small boy dodging right and left in front of the wiggling machine found himself beneath the panting Dangerfield.

"Are you hurt?"

"No I'm not."

"Are you sure?"

"No I'm not hurt."

"I'm very sorry, little boy. Must rush. Here, you can have this damn bike as a present, before I get killed on it."

The child left standing in the middle of the street, staring after the man who took off his hat and flung it behind the railings and bundled up his coat which followed it, opening, fluttering down.

Through this Cuffe Street. Up Aungier. Flat out. I'll keep up the pace. Get down this alley here and get through all these backyards. Walking between the white walls and piss smells. Don't want to be trapped either.

Dangerfield walked swiftly through the labyrinth of lanes into a little square with a lamp standard and more children. Stepped into a doorway and waited. No one behind. A little girl dragging a boy by the hair in the gutter. Kid screaming and kicking his legs. Bare feet swollen and cut. Another boy comes out of the house with a bundle of newspapers yelling for her to leave him alone and he gives her a punch on the arm and she kicks him in the knee and he grabs her and throws her down. She claws and scratches at his eyes and he bends her arms back and she spits in his face.

Sebastian leaves his doorway and walks slowly out the lane. Navigating widely and back and around and coming out along these terraced, red brick houses each with a polished knocker and curtains and little precious things at the first floor windows. Straight out this road I can see the Dublin Mountains with evening sun on them and I wish I were away out there with a massive wall built all round me. Into the tree lined street. Crossing over smartly. Slamming the little gate. Down the steps. Rap, rap. Wait. Silence, rap, rap. My God, my dear Chris, don't leave me out here for them to get me.

"Hello."

Voice behind him.

"Jesus."

"What's happened to you?"

Chris carrying packages, her face wreathed with concern as she came down the steps behind him.

"Let me in."

"Hold these. There's blood all down the back of your neck."

"A little misunderstanding."

"O dear. Have you been in a fight?"

"Little upset."

"Now tell me. Just what did happen?"

"All right. I'll go."

"Now don't be such a fool. Come in, sit down. Of course, you won't go. But you can't expect me to be all complacent when you just suddenly appear all covered in blood. How did this happen?"

"It happened."

"Don't talk nonsense. Hold still. I'll have to boil a

kettle and wash it. You've had too much to drink. Does it hurt?"

"No."

Chris in her drawer. Picking out the bottles. Iodine. Water in the kettle.

"Chris, I want you to tell me how I can get away from evil in this world. How to put down the sinners and raise the doers of good. I've been through a frightful evening. Indeed, my suffering has been acute and more. More than sin or evil or anything. I have arrived at the conclusion that these people on this island are bogus."

"You had a fight, didn't you?"

"Most ungentlemanly incident I think I've ever experienced."

"In a bar?"

"In a bar. The rudeness on this island is overwhelming."

"Well? How? Why?"

"I went to this public house for a quiet drink. Stone cold sober. Man seizes me by the arm and twists it—says get out—you're drunk. I said, I beg your pardon but I'm stone. Naturally I left under the maltreatment that was in it. Now I'm not an evil person, nor do I ever encourage any type of trouble. However I returned to this bar later, ordered another drink and they attacked me brutally. Disgraceful behavior. All on me like a pack of wolves. Trying to put me down and jump on me. It was only by employing the most elusive tactics that I succeeded in escaping with my very life. I have no doubts but that they are searching the city to visit me with more abuse."

"Now really."

"Come sit by me, Chris."

"No."

"Sit by me. I'm most upset."

"I'll do your head."

"Can I stay here tonight."

"Yes. I think you ought to have a bath."

"I've got to get out of this damn country. Honest to Christ."

"Any pennies?"

"None."

"You'll have to have a threepenny bath."

Helping him to take off his clothes. Out into this damp bathroom with the bathtub up on lion's paws and the cold sticky floor. In blub, gurgle slub dub glub. Foamy white face, no one to recognize me. Forever to walk backwards in the streets. The yellow light and green cracked ceiling. All last year you were in here in the tub while I was haunted and sad on Howth.

"Come away with me, Chris."

"You've had too much to drink. Say that when you're less confused."

"What? I say, confused."

"Turn around and let me dry your back."

"I want you to."

"I just can't suddenly decide something like that."

"You want to?"

"Where? And your wife and child?"

"We'll all manage."

"And your degree."

"Have to wait till I can regain my senses. I am in an awkward position."

"You are."

"You're giving me the evil treatment. Now I don't deserve that."

"Pull the light. I'll make you some chocolate."

No way out except the big way. I have put myself into a most unfortunate position. I hope to God that they don't catch me and put me in prison. They saw me ride madly through all the streets of Dublin. Please don't put me in Mountjoy prison, unless I'm given charge of the library. To be married to you, my dear Chris. But what has confounded me is blood. I was such a believer in blood, establishing the dynasty of Dangerfield, honorable kings of kingdoms and I have gotten as far as 1 Mohammed where the shit falls from the ceiling in a most sickening way and the bread is a week old and the tea like iron filings. I desire to be away in a more civilized country. What's to happen to me when I am old. And bent and busted.

Chris bringing two white cups to the table. She is all undressed wearing a robe. My head feels better. And she fills the hot water bottle. I can only say roll up the carpet of the earth and put it away till next summer, things will be better then. We two in the bed together. I think this is the only peace I have had for years. My dear Chris, to put my hand on your bare arse is such a pleasure. And to touch and feel you're near, for both of us are protection. All together in here. And we are, aren't we? Let us pray. To St. Jude for the impossible or is it allowed to pray for an orgasm?

[1955]

SOME HEADY PHRASES ON WINE

Art Buchwald

The problem of besting your friends at wine talk becomes increasingly difficult. It isn't enough to drink wines—you must be able to talk about them, if not intelligently, at least at length. Alexis Lichine, who wrote a book called "Wines of France," and who is up to his neck in the wine business, has given us some provocative phrases that can be used at the dinner table, either in your own home or as a guest in the home of a friend.

If you're serving wine in your own home Mr. Lichine advises you to be very modest. When the bottle is put on the table, apologize to your guests. "I'll have to beg your pardon," you might say, "but this is a small, red wine, inconsequential, with hardly any character." If your guests don't contradict you, start building slowly. After tasting it, remark to some one, "In spite of everything, I do believe it has some breed, even if it hasn't hit its pinnacle." If no one takes the bait, go a peg higher. "You know something, I believe this wine is declaring itself. Why yes, it certainly is. It does have manifestations of greatness at that." By this time, if your remarks still go unheeded, let out all stops. "The French consider this wine as one of their most magnificent sovereigns. They laughingly call it the Napoleon of Burgundies. It's a pity it has to be wasted on such clods."

Drinking wine in some one else's home is a much easier problem. The host is always looking for compliments and if you're not careful, some of the sillier people at the table may start giving them.

The thing to remember is always be polite. After tasting the wine a comment like this might be used, "Yes, it does have a pleasing shimmer. Isn't it too bad the nose doesn't live up to the color for it could have been a big, stout boy." Don't let up just because you've won the first engagement. You could continue by saying, "How sad it didn't come from noble soil, because I'm sure it might have taken on a prestige of its own. Yes, I've seen it happen, time and time again, with underprivileged wines." Or if you wish, "It's provocative, I'm sure, but I wouldn't dare put it up against a Haut Brion." Or, "What a delightful name. It almost tastes domestic in flavor."

When speaking of vintages, never refer to a wine as 1935 or 1936. Always drop the nineteen and refer to them as thirty-fours, thirty-fives, thirty-nines, etc. Learn the names of a few rare wines and throw them around as much as you can. If you can associate them with a good French restaurant, it always helps. For example, never say, "I like a Margaux." It's much better to reminisce, "I remember a Margaux I once had at the Grand Vefour in forty-six. What a noble lunch that was."

Never refer to "wine, woman and song" in front of connoisseurs. Next to wine, the other two are so inferior they should not be mentioned in the same breath.

It may be useful when talking about wine to know that Bordeaux comes in slim bottles and Burgundy in squat ones. This always impresses.

When ordering wines in restaurants, study the card for a long time even if you don't understand what you're reading. Cluck occasionally, and then turn to the sommelier and ask him to advise you on what to order. Never accept his first suggestion. He is testing you, and you don't want to lose face.

Always carry a vintage chart with you. If you're not sure of the best wine years, take the wine card to the washroom and check it against your vintage chart.

When drinking champagne, always make a remark about the bubbles. You can either take the side that you like the bubbles, or that you're against them. Our favorite line on this subject is, "I like champagne—because it always tastes like my foot's asleep."

[1954]

CANDY

Terry Southern
& Mason Hoffenberg

There was only one tree on Grove Street. This was the sort of thing Candy was quick to notice, and to love. "Look," she would say softly, squeezing someone's hand. "Isn't it too *much!* I could just hug myself every time I pass it!"

And that was where she met the hunchback.

It was late one airless summer day, when the sky over Greenwich Village was the color of lead. It had just begun to rain, and Candy was standing back in a shallow doorway, waiting for her bus. Dreamily humming a little Elizabethan tune, feeling fresh and quietly joyful in her new mandarin rain-cloak, hugging it to her—she saw him. He was out in the midst of the downpour, leaning against the tree, staring into the window display of the men's shop on the corner. He was standing very still, though from time to time there seemed to be a slight movement of his back, as if he might be consciously pressing his hump against the tree.

Candy's humming softened as she watched him, and her heart beat a little faster. *Oh, the fullness of it!* she thought, *the terrible, beautiful fullness of life!* And a great mass of feeling rose in her throat at the pity she felt for her father so shut away from it all, never to know life, never even to suspect what it was all about. She put her arms around her delightful body and hugged herself, so glad at being alive, really alive, and her eyes brimmed with shimmering gratitude.

Just then two boys passed the corner, dark coats turned up, heads half hidden out of the rain. One of them noticed the hunchback and gave a derisive snort:

"Wha'cha doin', Mac—gittin' yer nuts off?"

He kept nudging his companion, who wouldn't even bother to look.

"The guy's gittin' his *nuts* off fer chrissake!" he shouted again as they walked on.

The hunchback gazed after them oddly.

"Rubatubdub!" he said. "Rubadubtub!"

Candy hadn't heard either one of them distinctly, but there was no mistaking the tone of contempt, the obvious effort to hurt and humiliate. "The ignorant fools!" she said half aloud, and gave a little stamp of impatience. At that moment the bus rounded the corner beyond; she frowned as she watched it approach, but just before it reached her, she took a deep breath and walked away from the stop, then casually over to where the hunchback was standing.

"*Hi!*" she said, giving him a wonderfully warm smile and tossing back the hood of her cloak to feel the fresh rain on her face. . . . Wasn't it just too much, she thought joyfully, standing here in the rain, in Greenwich Village, talking to a hunchback—when she *should* have been at her job ten minutes ago! . . . She considered the explanation she would have to give, the attempt to make them understand, and she was so happy and proud of herself she could have wept.

"That's *my* tree, you know," she said instead, smiling like a mischievous child, then laughing gaily at her own foolishness. "I pretend that it is," she admitted, almost shyly. "The *only* tree on Grove Street! Oh, I do love it so!" She leaned forward and touched it gently, half closing her eyes, and then she gave the hunchback another tender smile.

The shop on this corner of Grove was a man's underwear shop, and the hunchback's eyes devoured another crotch or two before he looked up. He was also smiling. He supposed she was a policewoman. *"Rubatubdub!"* he said, agitating his hump vigorously against the tree. Getting run in was part of his kick.

"Three men in a tub!" cried Candy, laughing in marvel at their immediate rapport. How simple! she thought. How wonderfully, beautifully simple the important things are! And how it had so completely escaped her father! She would have given twenty years of her life to have shared the richness of this moment with her father— he who had said that poems were "impractical"! The poor darling dummy! Why *only* a poem could capture it! Only a poem could trap the elusiveness, the light-like subtlety, the vapor-edge of a really big thing, and lead it, coax it past . . . a poem, or music perhaps . . . yes, of course, music. And she began to hum softly, swaying her body a little, her fingers distractedly caressing the tree. She felt very relaxed with the hunchback.

And he was still smiling too—but that first gray glimmer of hope had died from his eyes, and they narrowed a bit now as he decided, quite simply, that she was a nut.

"Hungry," he said, pointing to his mouth, *"hungry."*

"Oh!" cried Candy, suddenly remembering and she reached into the pocket of her cloak and took out a small paper bag. It was a bag of bread crumbs; she carried it often for pigeons in Washington Square. "I have this," she said, her wide eyes beautifully blue and ingenuous. She helped herself first, to show that it wasn't mere charity, but rather a human experience, simple, warm, and shared.

There was something disconcerting though in the way this hunchback sniggered, rolling his eyes, and squirmed against the tree, wiping his mouth with the back of his hand; but, after a moment, he took some of the crumbs too.

"Rubatubdub!" he said.

Candy laughed. She heard a wisdom and complex symbology in the hunchback's simple phrases. It was as though she were behind the scenes of something like the Dadaist movement, even creatively a part of it. This was the way things happened, she thought, the really big things, things that ten years later change the course of history, just this way, on the street corners of the Village; and here she was, a part of it. How incredibly ironic that her father would have thought she was "wasting her time!" The notion made her throat tighten and her heart rise up in sorrow for him.

"You got quarter, lady?" asked the hunchback then, nodding his head in anticipation. He held out his hand, but Candy was already shaking her curls defensively and fumbling in her purse.

"No, I don't think I have a *cent,* darn it! Here's an Athenian florin," she said, holding a lump of silver, then dropping it back into the purse, "550 B.C. . . . *that* won't do us any good, will it? Not unless we're Sappho and Pythagoras and don't know it!" And she looked up, closing her purse and shaking her head, happily, as though not having any money herself would actually make them closer.

"*Are* you Pythagoras?" she asked gaily.

"You get your rubadub, don't you, lady?" muttered the hunchback as he started shuffling away. "*Fuckashitpiss! Fuckashitpiss! Rubadub, rubadub!*"

This struck Candy with such anxiety that for a moment she was speechless. She could not bear the idea of his going away angry, and also in the back of her mind was the pride she would feel if, in a few days, she could be walking down the street with Ted and Harold, or with one of the people from International House, and the hunchback would speak to her by name; they might even stop and chat a bit, and she would introduce him:

"Ted, this is my friend Derek," or whatever; it could certainly be as important as Blind Battersea, the sightless beggar in Washington Park, being able to recognize Ted's voice.

"Listen," she cried, hurrying after him, "if you don't mind potluck, we could have something at my place— it's just past the corner here—I know there are some eggs. . . ."

When Candy had slipped out of her cloak and kicked off her shoes, she went into the bathroom. "Won't be a minute," she said, and very soon she reappeared, rubbing her hair with a towel, fluffing it out, her head back, eyes half closed for the moment as she stood there in the middle of the room.

"I don't know which is best," she said with a luxurious sigh, "the freshness of rain . . . or the warmth of fire."

She had changed into a loose flannel shirt and a pair of tight-fitting faded bluejeans which were rolled up almost to the knee. She had another towel draped across her shoulder, and she laid this on the arm of the hunchback's chair as she crossed the room.

"Take off some of your things if you want," she said airily, "let them dry by the radiator," and she sat on the edge of the couch opposite him and rubbed her feet with the towel, doing this carefully and impersonally, as though they were pieces of priceless china which belonged to someone else, yet silhouetting the white curve of her bare legs against the black corduroy couch-cover, and exclaiming genially: "My feet are soaked! Aren't yours?" She didn't wait for an answer, nor seemed to expect one, only wanting to maintain a casual chatter to put the hunchback at ease; she took care not to look at him directly, as she stood up and crossed the room again, indicating with a gesture the magazine stand near his chair: "There's a *PR* and *Furioso* there—if you feel like light reading. I'm afraid there's not much else at the moment—I'll just get us a drink." And she disappeared then into the tiny kitchen.

The hunchback had been sniggering and squirming about in the chair, and now finally he picked up the towel and wiped his face, then blew his nose into it and spat several times.

"Rubatubtub!" he muttered.

Candy's gay laugh rang from the kitchen.

"Wish we had something stronger," she called out, "we could use it after that rain." Then she came in with a large bottle of Chianti and two glasses already filled, and set these on the table. "Help yourself to more," she said, taking a sip of hers. "Umm, good," she said, and went back into the kitchen, "won't be a minute . . . well, not more than *five,* anyway." She had turned on the phono—some Gregorian chants—and hummed along with the music now as she busied herself, coming in and out, setting the table, and keeping up a spritely monologue the while.

The hunchback had a sip of the wine and spat it in the towel.

Through the open door of the kitchen, Candy could be seen moving about, and now she was bending over to put something into the oven. In the tight jeans, her round little buttocks looked so firm and ripe that any straight-thinking man would have rushed in at once to squeeze and bite them; but the hunchback's mind was filled with freak-ish thoughts. From an emotional standpoint, he would rather have been in the men's room down at Jack's Bar on the Bowery, eating a piece of urine-soaked bread while thrusting his hump against someone from the Vice Squad. And yet, though he had decided that she was nutty (and because of this she was of no use to his ego), he was also vaguely aware that she was a mark; and, in an obscure, obstacle-strewn way, he was trying to think about this now: *how to get the money.* He wasn't too good at it, however, for his sincerity of thought was not direct enough: he didn't really feel he *needed* money, but rather that he *should* feel he needed it. It was perhaps the last vestige of normalcy in the hunchback's values; it only cropped up now and then.

"Onion omelet," Candy announced with a flourish as she entered, "hope you like tarragon and lots of garlic," and she put it on the table. "Looks good, doesn't it?" She felt she could say this last with a certain innocent candor, because her friends assured her she was a very good cook.

Aside from an occasional grunt and snort, the hunchback kept silent throughout the meal and during Candy's lively commentary, while into his image-laden brain now and then shot the primal questions: *"Where? No kill! How? Without kill! Where?"*

This silence of his impressed Candy all the more, making her doubly anxious to win his approval. "Oh, but here I'm talking away a mile, and you can't get in a single word!" She beamed, and nodded with a show of wisdom. "Or isn't it really that there's nothing to say—'would it have been worth while *after all,* et cetera, et cetera.' Yes, *I* know . . . oh, there's the tea now. *Tea!* Good night, *I'm* still on Eliot—the darling old fuddy, don't you *love* him? It's coffee, of course. Espresso. I won't be a minute. . . . Have some of the Camembert, not too *bien fait,* I'm afraid, but . . ." She rushed out to the kitchen, still holding her napkin, while the hunchback sat quietly, munching his bread. It was hardly the first time he had been involved in affairs of this sort.

When the darling girl returned, she suggested they

move over to the couch to have their coffee. There she sat close beside him and leafed through a book of Blake's reproductions.

"Aren't they a *groove*," she was saying, "they're *so* funny! Most people don't get it at all!" She looked up at the wall opposite, where another print was hanging, and said gleefully: "And don't you just love *that* one? The details, I mean, did you ever look at it closely? Let me get it."

The print was hanging by a wire placed high, and Candy had to reach. She couldn't quite get it at first, and for a long moment she was standing there, lithe and lovely, stretching upward, standing on the tiptoes of one foot, the other out like a ballet-dancer's. As she strained higher, she felt the sinews of her calf rounding firmly and the edge of her flannel shirt lifting gently above her waist and upward across her bare back, while the muscles of her darling little buttocks tightened and thrust out taut beneath the jeans. Oh, I *shouldn't!* she thought, making another last effort to reach the print. What if he thinks I'm . . . well, it's *my* fault, darn it!

As it happened, the hunchback *was* watching her and, with the glimpse of her bare waist, it occurred to him suddenly, as though the gray sky itself had fallen, that, as for the other girls who had trafficked with him, what they had wanted was to be ravenously desired—to be so overwhelmingly physically needed that, despite their every effort to the contrary for a real and spiritual rapport, their beauty so powerfully, undeniably asserted itself as to reduce the complex man to simple beast . . . who must be fed.

By the time Candy had the print down and had reached the couch with it, the eyes of the hunchback were quite changed; they seemed to be streaked with red now, and they were very bright. The precious girl noticed it at once, and she was a little flustered as she sat down, speaking rapidly, pointing to the print: "Isn't this too *much?* Look at this figure, here in the corner, most people don't even . . ." She broke off for a moment to cough and blush terribly as the hunchback's eyes devoured her, glistening. In an effort to regain composure, she touched her lovely curls and gave a little toss of her head. "What *can* he be thinking?" she asked herself. "Well, it's my own fault, darn it!" The small eyes of the hunchback blazed; he was thinking of *money.* "I love you!" he said then quickly, the phrase sounding odd indeed.

"Oh, darling, *don't* say that!" said Candy, imploring, as though she had been quite prepared, yet keeping her eyes down on the book.

"I want very much!" he said, touching her arm at the elbow.

She shivered just imperceptibly and covered his hand with her own. "You mustn't say that," she said with softness and dignity.

"I want fuck you!" he said, putting his hand on her pert left breast.

She clasped his hand, holding it firmly, as she turned to him, her eyes closed, a look of suffering on her face. "No, darling, please," she murmured and she was quite firm.

"I want fuck—suck you!" he said, squeezing the breast while she felt the sweet little nipple reaching out like a tiny mushroom.

She stood up abruptly, putting her hands to her face. "Don't. Please don't," she said. She stood there a moment, then walked to the window. "Oh why must it be like this?" she beseeched the dark sky of the failing day. "Why? Why?" She turned and was about to repeat it, but the voice of the hunchback came first.

"Is because of *this?*" he demanded. "Because of *this?*" He was sitting there with a wretched expression on his face, and one arm raised and curled behind his head, pointing at his hump.

Candy came forward quickly, like a nurse in emergency. "*No,* you poor darling, of course it isn't! *No, no,*" and the impetus of her flight carried her down beside him again and put him in her arms. "You silly darling!" She closed her eyes, leaning her face against his as she stroked his head. "I hadn't even noticed," she said.

"Why, then?" he wanted to know. "*Why?*"

Now that she had actually touched him, she seemed more at ease. "*Why?*" she sighed. "Oh, I don't know. Girls are like that, never quite knowing what they want—or need. Oh, I don't know, I want it to be *perfect,* I guess."

"Because of *this,*" repeated the hunchback, shrugging heavily.

"No, you darling," she cooed, insisting, closed-eyed again, nudging his cheek with her nose, "no, no, no. What earthly *difference* does it make! I have blue eyes—you have that. What possible difference does it make?"

"*Why?*" he demanded, reaching up under her shirt to grasp one of her breasts, then suddenly pulling her brassiere up and her shoulder back, and thrusting forward to cover the breast with his mouth. Candy sobbed, "*Oh, darling, no,*" but allowed her head to recline gently against the couch. "Why does it have to be like this?" she pleaded. "Why? Oh, I know it's my own fault, darn it." And she let him kiss and suck her breast, until the nipple became terribly taut and she began to tingle all down through her precious tummy, then she pulled his head away, cradling it in her arms, her own eyes shimmering with tears behind a brave smile. "No, darling," she implored, "*please* . . . not now."

"Because of *this,*" said the hunchback bitterly.

"No, no, no," she cried, closing her eyes and hugging the head to her breast, holding his cheek against it, but trying to keep his mouth from the proud little nipple, "no, no, *not* because of that!"

"I want!" said the hunchback, with one hand on her hip now undoing the side buttons of her jeans; then he swiftly forced the hand across the panty sheen of her rounded tummy and down into the sweet damp.

"Oh, darling, no!" cried the girl, but it was too late, without making a scene, for anything to be done; his stubby fingers were rolling the little clitoris like a marble in oil. Candy leaned back in resignation, her heart too big to deprive him of this if it meant so much. With her head closed-eyed, resting again on the couch, she would endure it as long as she could. But, before she reached the saturation point, he had nuzzled his face down from her breast across her bare stomach and into her lap, bending his arm forward to force down her jeans and panties as he did, pulling at them on the side with his other hand.

"No, no, darling!" she sighed, but he soon had them down below her knees, at least enough so to replace his fingers with his tongue.

It means so much to him, Candy kept thinking, *so* much, as he meanwhile got her jeans and panties down completely so that they dangled now from one slender ankle as he adjusted her legs and was at last on the floor himself in front of her, with her legs around his neck and his mouth very deep inside the fabulous honeypot.

"If it means so much," Candy kept repeating to herself, until she didn't think she could bear it another second, and she wrenched herself free, saying *"Darling, oh darling,"* and seized his head in her hands with a great show of passion.

"Oh, why?" she begged, holding his face in her hands, looking at him mournfully. "Why?"

"I need fuck you!" said the hunchback huskily. He put his face against the upper softness of her marvelous bare leg. Small, strange sounds came from his throat.

"Oh, darling, darling," the girl keened pitifully, "I can't bear your crying." She sighed, and smiled tenderly, stroking his head.

"I *think* we'd better go into the bedroom," she said then, her manner suddenly prim and efficient.

In the bathroom, standing before the glass, Candy finished undressing—unbuttoning her shirt, slowly, carefully, a lamb resigned to the slaughter, dropping the shirt to the floor, and taking off her brassiere, gradually revealing her nakedness to herself, with a little sigh, almost of wistful regret, at how *very* lovely she was, and at how her nipples grew and stood out like cherrystones, as they always did when she watched herself undress. How he *wants* me! she thought. Well, it's my own fault, darn it! And she tried to imagine the raging lust that the hunchback felt for her as she touched her curls lightly. Then she cast a last glimpse at herself in the glass, blushing at her own loveliness, and trembling slightly at the very secret notion of this beauty-and-beast sacrifice, she went back into the bedroom.

The hunchback was lying naked, curled on his side like a big foetus, when Candy appeared before him, standing for a moment in full lush radiance, a naked angel being the supreme gift. Then, she got into bed quickly, under the sheet, almost soundlessly, saying, *"Darling, darling,"* and cuddling him to her at once, while he, his head filled with the most freakish thoughts imaginable—all about tubs of living and broken toys, every manner of excrement, scorpions, steelwool, pig-masks, odd metal harness, etc.—tried desperately to pry into the images a single reminder: the *money!*

"Do you want to kiss me some more, darling?" asked the girl with deadly soft seriousness, her eyes wide, searching his own as one would a child's. Then she sighed and lay back, slowly taking the sheet from her, again to make him the gift of all her wet, throbbing treasures, as he, glazed-eyed and grunting, slithered down beside her.

"Don't hurt me, darling," she murmured, as in a dream, while he parted the exquisitely warm round thighs with his great head, his mouth opening the slick lips all sugar and glue, and his quick tongue finding her pink candy clit at once.

"Oh, darling, darling," she said, stroking his head gently, watching him, a tender courageous smile on her face.

The hunchback put his hands under her, gripping the foam-rubber balls of her buttocks, and sucked and nibbled her tiny clit with increasing vigor. Candy closed her eyes and gradually raised her legs, straining gently upward now, dropping her arms back by her head, one to each side, pretending they were pinioned there, writhing slowly, sobbing—until she felt she was no longer giving, but was on the verge of taking, and, as with an effort, she broke her hands from above her and grasped the hunchback's head and lifted it to her mouth, coming forward to meet him, kissing him deeply. "Come inside me, darling," she whispered urgently, "I want you *inside* me!"

The hunchback, his brain seething with pure strangeness, hardly heard her. He had forgotten about the money, but did know that *something* was at stake, and his head was about to burst in trying to recall what it was. Inside his mind was like a gigantic landslide of black eels, billions of them, surging past, one of which held the answer. His job: *catch it!* Catch it, and chew off the top of its head; and there, in the gurgling cup, would be . . . the *message:* "You have forgotten about . . . ?"

But which eel was it? While his eyes grew wilder and rolled back until only the whites showed, Candy, thinking that he was beside himself with desire for her, covered his face with sweet wet kisses, until he suddenly went stiff in her arms as his racing look stopped abruptly on the floor near the bed: it was a coat hanger, an ordinary wire coat hanger, which had fallen from the closet, and the hunchback flung himself out of the bed and onto the floor, clutching the hanger to him feverishly. Then, as in a fit of bitter triumph, he twisted it savagely into a single length of coiled black wire, and gripping it so tightly that his entire body shook for a moment, he lunged forward, one end of it locked between his teeth. *He thought it was the eel.*

Candy had started up, half sitting now, one hand instinctively to her pert, pulsating breast.

"Darling, what is it?" she cried. "Darling, you *aren't* going to . . ."

The hunchback slowly rose, as one recovered from a seizure of apoplexy, seeming to take account of his surroundings anew, and, just as he had learned from the eel's head that the forgotten issue was money, so too he believed now that the girl wanted to be beaten.

"*Why,* darling?" pleaded Candy, curling her lovely legs as the hunchback slowly raised the black wire snake above his head. "*Why? Why?*" she cried.

And as he began to strike her across the back of her legs, she sobbed, "Oh, why, darling, why?" her long round limbs twisting, as she turned and writhed, her arms back beside her head as before, moving too except at the wrist where they were as stiff as though clamped there with steel, and she was saying: "Yes! *Hurt* me! Yes, yes! Hurt me as *they* have hurt you!" and now her ankles as well seemed secured, shackled to the spot, as she lay, spread-eagled, sobbing piteously, straining against her invisible bonds, her lithe round body arching upward, hips circling slowly, mouth wet, nipples taut, her teeny piping clitoris distended and throbbing, and her eyes glistening like fire, as she devoured all the penitence for each injustice ever done to hunchbacks of the world; and as it continued she slowly opened her eyes, that all the world might see the tears there—but instead she herself saw, through the rise and fall of the wire lash—the hunchback's white gleaming hump! The *hump,* the white, unsunned forever, radish-root white of hump, and it struck her, more sharply than the wire whip, as something she had seen before—the naked, jutting buttocks, upraised in a sexual thrust, not a thrust of taking, but of *giving,* for it had been an image in a hospital room mirror, of her own precious buttocks, naked and upraised, gleaming white, and thrusting downwards, as she had been made to do in giving herself to her Uncle Jack!

With a wild impulsive cry, she shrieked: *"Give me your hump!"*

The hunchback was startled for a moment, not comprehending.

"Your hump, your hump!" cried the girl. "GIVE ME YOUR HUMP!"

The hunchback hesitated, and then lunged headlong toward her, burying his hump between Candy's leg as she hunched wildly, pulling open her little labias in an absurd effort to get it in her.

"Your hump! Your hump!" she kept crying, scratching and clawing at it now.

"Fuck! Shit! Piss!" she screamed. "Cunt! Cock! Crap! Prick! Kike! Nigger! Wop! *Hump!* HUMP!" and she teetered on the blazing peak of pure madness for an instant . . . and then dropped down, slowly, through gray and grayer clouds into a deep, soft, black night.

When Candy awoke she was alone. She lay back, thinking over the events of the afternoon. Well, it's my own fault, darn it, she sighed, then smiled a little smile of forgiveness at herself—but this suddenly changed to a small frown, and she sat up in bed, cross as a pickle. "*Darn* it!" she said aloud, and with real feeling, for she had forgotten to have them exchange names.

[1958]

MOTEL CHRONICLES

Sam Shepard

On the train that I love so much. The train they named
and re-named; first, according to the terrain it crossed,
then, later, to jibe with a corporate sense of anonymity.
The train remains the same. And all the same feelings
swell up in me on this train. Same wonders. Same heart-
breaking hunger for the land outside the window. I'd live
on a train if someone gave me one.

On this same train I'm sitting down in the diner.
Scanning. Pretending to read the menu. A Tuesday Weld-
type-of-blonde girl, maybe fifteen, in bare feet is reading a
thick green book and dawdling with a salad. She keeps
looking straight at me then back to the book. I can't take
my eyes off her feet. It's her feet that remind me of
Tuesday Weld more than her hair. It's her feet that take
me back to an early T.V. Talk Show where Tuesday Weld
appeared in bare feet and a full skirt and the interviewer (I
think it was David Susskind) spent the whole time putting
her down for having bare feet on his show and how this
was a strong indication of her neurotic immaturity and
need for attention. I fell in love with Tuesday Weld on that
show. I thought she was the Marlon Brando of women.

This girl keeps staring at me over her thick green book
and I'm getting all constricted around the throat. She's
wearing one of those blue stretchy kind of tops with no
straps. The kind you just pull straight down and everything becomes instantly available. She seems to be taking a
long time to finish her salad.

I move over to her table and ask her what she's reading. "The History of American Suicide," she says.

I say, "Are you a student of Suicide?"

She says, "No."

I say, "Oh."

One thing leads to another and we wind up in her stateroom. She's only fifteen, I'm thinking. I'm only nineteen. Fifteen and nineteen. That means when I was four, she was nowhere. She says she's a Mormon. She says her Daddy's picking her up in Salt Lake. *(I'M PICTURING HER DADDY IN A BROAD-BRIMMED BLACK HAT, BLACK SUIT, BLACK STRING TIE, SEATED IN A BUGGY BEHIND A BLACK MULE WITH A WHIP IN ONE HAND, WAITING AT THE TRAIN STATION. SEA GULLS SLOWLY CIRCLING ABOVE HIS HEAD.)*

She unfolds the bed from the wall. She thinks it's a joke. The bed falls into place leaving no room to stand. The train jerks. Her top comes down even easier than I imagined. She tells me she can't "do" and I've never heard this expression before so I say, "do what?" We "do" all the way from Winnemucca through the Great Salt Lake Desert. It's a lot like crossing the ocean at night. A sea train. Salt glows white through the window. She says she'll never be able to face her boyfriend again.

When the train pulls into Salt Lake I watch her leap from the metal steps of the coach straight through a cloud of steam. I hear her bare feet hit the gravel but she's gone. There's a strong smell of steel in the air. Lights from the station platform. Red Caps pushing baggage carts. The steam thins out and a street appears in the distance. I have an itch to follow the street. Just abandon ship and follow her, but she's nowhere in sight. "Tuesday!" I yell out to the Salt Lake City night. "Tuesday, don't leave me!"

Back in my seat, the train rolls. I suddenly start having vivid premonitions that she'll spill the beans to her Daddy. I expect retaliation at every stop. Doors bursting open. *(HER DADDY HAS TAKEN ON A STERLING HAYDEN FACE NOW AND CARRIES A TWELVE-GAUGE SHOTGUN. I'M TERRIFIED THE TRAIN WILL STOP IN SOME REMOTE OUTPOST AND THE CONDUCTOR WILL HAND ME OVER TO THE VINDICTIVE FATHER. I'LL BE CARRIED INTO THE DESERT AND BEHEADED. I'LL BE MUTI-LATED LIKE OSIRIS AND THIS BLONDE LITTLE ISIS WILL COME SEARCHING FOR MY PARTS. PIECING ME BACK TOGETHER. IT WILL TAKE HER YEARS TO FIND ALL MY MEMBERS AND STILL MY MOST PRIVATE ORGANS WILL HAVE ESCAPED HER, FLOATING DOWN THE COL-ORADO RIVER DEEP INTO MEXICO. SHE'LL FOLLOW THE RIVER, MOURNING MY FRAC-TURED CORPSE. HOLDING MY SEVERED HEAD UP TO THE MOON AND MOANING AS SHE FLOATS. THE SOUND OF HER LAMENT WILL FILL THE GRAND CANYON.)*

At 1:30 A.M. I get off in Missouri. I'm due for Chicago in the morning but I can't stand to ride it out. At least on foot I'll have a chance. I find a phone booth by a corn field and call Illinois collect. My Grandmother answers. She's not glad to hear from me. She's not glad to be paying for this call. She can't picture where I am or why I'm calling. "I'm in a phone booth by a corn field in Missouri. Right near the Mississippi." She can't figure it out. I haven't seen her for seven years or even written her a letter. "I'm com-ing in to see you tomorrow. How's Grandpa?" She asks me if I realize what time it is. "Yeah, I'm sorry Grandma but I had to get off the train. I was afraid for my life."

I take a Greyhound into Chicago then hitch out to the country. The farm looks abandoned. A small stand of dried-up corn stalks by the house with dead crows that my Grandfather's shot hanging by their necks, tied with red rubber bands so they bounce slightly when the wind hits them. My Grandpa's theory is that they function as scarecrows to the living crows.

My Grandpa sits exactly as he's always sat—in a hole of his sofa wrapped in crocheted blankets facing the T.V. He's like a skeleton now. He likes the Hamm's Beer commercials. "The Land of Sky Blue Waters." The little cartoon Beaver that jumps around on top of the waterfall and sings the jingle. He thinks Truman was our greatest President and writes political rebuffs to the Chicago papers, signing them "Plain Dirt Farmer." He predicts "a Nigger in the White House" by 1970. He's a staunch fan of the Chicago Cubs. He tells me I never should have abandoned baseball. "You could've had a career in the Majors," he says. "Not a bad life. Gettin' paid to play ball." He smokes and drinks continuously and spits blood into a stand-up brass ash tray like you see in the lobbies of old hotels. Sometimes he coughs so violently that his whole body doubles over and he can't catch his breath for a long long time. His world is circumscribed around the sofa. Everything he needs is within a three-foot reach. The T.V. is only on for the baseball. When the game ends my Grandmother comes in and turns it off. She does it right on cue. She can hear when the game ends from any room in the house. She has great ears.

When everyone's asleep I wander around in the room upstairs staring at all the photographs of my Uncles. The Uncle who died in a motel room on his wedding night. His wife who died with him. The Uncle who lost a leg at the age of ten. The Uncle who married into the Chicago

Mafia. The Uncle who cut timber in the Great North Woods. The Uncle who drove for Bekins. The Uncle who raised Springer Spaniels. All the Uncles who carry the bones of my Grandpa's face.

I fall back on the bed. "Fifteen and nineteen," I'm thinking. "Fifteen and nineteen." A train whistles way off. Cicadas buzz. I can still hear her feet hit the gravel.

[1980]

CONCERNING TOBACCO

Mark Twain

As concerns tobacco, there are many superstitions. And the chiefest is this—that there is a *standard* governing the matter, whereas there is nothing of the kind. Each man's own preference is the only standard for him, the only one which he can accept, the only one which can command him. A congress of all the tobacco-lovers in the world could not elect a standard which would be binding upon you or me, or would even much influence us.

The next superstition is that a man has a standard of his own. He hasn't. He thinks he has, but he hasn't. He thinks he can tell what he regards as a good cigar from what he regards as a bad one—but he can't. He goes by the brand, yet imagines he goes by the flavor. One may palm off the worst counterfeit upon him; if it bears his brand he will smoke it contentedly and never suspect.

Children of twenty-five, who have seven years of experience, try to tell me what is a good cigar and what isn't. Me, who never learned to smoke, but always smoked; me, who came into the world asking for a light.

No one can tell me what is a good cigar—for me. I am the only judge. People who claim to know say that I smoke the worst cigars in the world. They bring their own cigars when they come to my house. They betray an unmanly terror when I offer them a cigar; they tell lies and hurry away to meet engagements which they have not made when they are threatened with the hospitalities of my box. Now then, observe what superstition, assisted by a man's reputation, can do. I was to have twelve personal friends to supper one night. One of them was as notorious for costly and elegant cigars as I was for cheap and devilish ones. I called at his house and when no one was looking borrowed a double handful of his very choicest; cigars which cost him forty cents apiece and bore red-and-gold labels in sign of their nobility. I removed the labels and put the cigars into a box with my favorite brand on it—a brand which those people all knew, and which cowed them as men are cowed by an epidemic. They took these cigars when offered at the end of the supper, and lit them and sternly struggled with them—in dreary silence, for hilarity died when the fell brand came into view and started around—but their fortitude held for a short time only; then they made excuses and filed out, treading on one another's heels with indecent eagerness; and in the morning when I went out to observe results the cigars lay all between the front door and the gate. All except one— that one lay in the plate of the man from whom I had cabbaged the lot. One or two whiffs was all he could stand. He told me afterward that some day I would get shot for giving people that kind of cigars to smoke.

Am I certain of my own standard? Perfectly; yes, absolutely—unless somebody fools me by putting my brand on some other kind of cigar; for no doubt I am like the rest, and know my cigar by the brand instead of by the flavor. However, my standard is a pretty wide one and covers a good deal of territory. To me, almost any cigar is good that nobody else will smoke, and to me almost all cigars are bad that other people consider good. Nearly any cigar will do me, except a Havana. People think they hurt my feelings when they come to my house with their life preservers on—I mean, with their own cigars in their pockets. It is an error; I take care of myself in a similar way. When I go into danger—that is, into rich people's houses, where, in the nature of things, they will have high-tariff cigars, red-and-gilt girdled and nested in a rosewood box along with a damp sponge, cigars which develop a dismal black ash and burn down the side and smell, and will grow hot to the fingers, and will go on growing hotter and hotter, and go on smelling more and more infamously and unendurably the deeper the fire tunnels down inside below the thimbleful of honest tobacco that is in the front end, the furnisher of it praising it all the time and telling you how much the deadly thing cost—yes, when I go into that sort of peril I carry my own defense along; I carry my own brand—twenty-seven cents a barrel—and I live to see my family again. I may seem to light his red-gartered cigar, but that is only for courtesy's sake; I smuggle it into my pocket for the poor, of whom I know many, and light one of my own; and while he praises it I join in, but when he says it cost forty-five cents I say nothing, for I know better.

However, to say true, my tastes are so catholic that I have never seen any cigar that I really could not smoke, except those that cost a dollar apiece. I have examined those and know that they are made of dog-hair, and not good dog-hair at that.

I have a thoroughly satisfactory time in Europe, for all over the Continent one finds cigars which not even the most hardened newsboys in New York would smoke. I brought cigars with me, the last time; I will not do that any more. In Italy, as in France, the Government is the only cigar-peddler. Italy has three or four domestic brands: the Minghetti, the Trabuco, the Virginia, and a very coarse one which is a modification of the Virginia. The Minghettis are large and comely, and cost three dollars and sixty cents a hundred; I can smoke a hundred in seven days and enjoy every one of them. The Trabucos suit me, too; I don't remember the price. But one has to learn to like the Virginia, nobody is born friendly to it. It looks like a rattail file, but smokes better, some think. It has a straw through it; you pull this out, and it leaves a flue, otherwise there would be no draught, not even as much as there is to a nail. Some prefer a nail at first. However, I like all the French, Swiss, German, and Italian domestic cigars, and have never cared to inquire what they are made of; and nobody would know, anyhow, perhaps. There is even a brand of European smoking-tobacco that I like. It is a brand used by the Italian peasants. It is loose and dry and black, and looks like tea-grounds. When the fire is applied it expands, and climbs up and towers above the pipe, and presently tumbles off inside of one's vest. The tobacco itself is cheap, but it raises the insurance. It is as I remarked in the beginning—the taste for tobacco is a matter of superstition. There are no standards—no real standards. Each man's preference is the only standard for him, the only one which he can accept, the only one which can command him.

[1917]

TROPIC OF CANCER

Henry Miller

Paris is like a whore. From a distance she seems ravishing, you can't wait until you have her in your arms. And five minutes later you feel empty, disgusted with yourself. You feel tricked.

I returned to Paris with money in my pocket—a few hundred francs, which Collins had shoved in my pocket just as I was boarding the train. It was enough to pay for a room and at least a week's good rations. It was more than I had had in my hands at one time for several years. I felt elated, as though perhaps a new life was opening before me. I wanted to conserve it too, so I looked up a cheap hotel over a bakery on the Rue du Château, just off the Rue de Vanves, a place that Eugene had pointed out to me once. A few yards away was the bridge that spans the Montparnasse tracks. A familiar quarter.

I could have had a room for a hundred francs a month, a room without any conveniences to be sure—without even a window—and perhaps I would have taken it, just to be sure of a place to flop for a while, had it not been for the fact that in order to reach this room I would have been obliged to first pass through the room of a blind man. The thought of passing his bed every night had a most depressing effect upon me. I decided to look elsewhere. I went over to the Rue Cels, just behind the cemetery, and I looked at a sort of rat trap there with balconies running around the courtyard. There were bird-cages suspended from the balcony too, all along the lower tier. A cheerful sight perhaps, but to me it seemed like the public ward in a hospital. The proprietor didn't seem to have all his wits either. I decided to wait for the night, to have a good look around, and then choose some attractive little joint in a quiet side street.

At dinnertime I spent fifteen francs for a meal, just about twice the amount I had planned to allot myself. That made me so wretched that I wouldn't allow myself to sit down for a coffee, even despite the fact that it had begun to drizzle. I would walk about a bit and then go quietly to bed, at a reasonable hour. I was already miserable, trying to husband my resources this way. I had never in my life done it; it wasn't in my nature.

Finally it began to come down in bucketsful. I was glad. That would give me the excuse I needed to duck somewhere and stretch my legs out. It was still too early to go to bed. I began to quicken my pace, heading back toward the Boulevard Raspail. Suddenly a woman comes up to me and stops me, right in the pouring rain. She wants to know what time it is. I told her I didn't have a watch. And then she bursts out, just like this: "Oh, my good sir, do you speak English by chance?" I nod my head. It's coming down in torrents now. "Perhaps, my dear good man, you would be so kind as to take me to a café. It is raining so and I haven't the money to sit down anywhere. You will excuse me, my dear sir, but you have such a kind face . . . I knew you were English right away." And with this she smiles at me, a strange, half-demented smile. "Perhaps you could give me a little advice, dear sir. I am all alone in the world . . . my God, it is terrible to have no money . . ."

This "dear sir" and "kind sir" and "my good man," etc., had me on the verge of hysteria. I felt sorry for her and yet I had to laugh. I did laugh. I laughed right in her face. And then she laughed too, a weird, high-pitched laugh, off-key, an altogether unexpected piece of cachinnation. I caught her by the arm and we made a bolt for it to the nearest café. She was still giggling when we entered the *bistro*. "My dear good sir," she began, "perhaps you think I am not telling you the truth. I am a good girl . . . I come of a good family. Only"—and here she gave me that wan, broken smile again—"only I am so misfortunate as not to have a place to sit down." At this I began to laugh again. I couldn't help it—the phrases she used, the strange accent, the crazy hat she had on, that demented smile. . . .

"Listen," I interrupted, "what nationality are you?"

"I'm English," she replied. "That is, I was born in Poland, but my father is Irish."

"So that makes you English?"

"Yes," she said, and she began to giggle again, sheepishly, and with a pretense of being coy.

"I suppose you know a nice little hotel where you could take me?" I said this, not because I had any intention of going with her, but just to spare her the usual preliminaries.

"Oh, my dear sir," she said, as though I had made the most grievous error, "I'm sure you don't mean that! I'm not that kind of a girl. You were joking with me, I can see that. You're so good . . . you have such a kind face. I would not dare to speak to a Frenchman as I did to you. They insult you right away. . . ."

She went on in this vein for some time. I wanted to break away from her. But she didn't want to be left alone. She was afraid—her papers were not in order. Wouldn't I be good enough to walk her to her hotel? Perhaps I could "lend" her fifteen or twenty francs, to quiet the *patron?* I walked her to the hotel where she said she was stopping and I put a fifty franc bill in her hand. Either she was very clever, or very innocent—it's hard to tell sometimes—but, at any rate, she wanted me to wait until she ran to the *bistro* for change. I told her not to bother. And with that she seized my hand impulsively and raised it to her lips. I was flabbergasted. I felt like giving her every damned thing I had. That touched me, that crazy little gesture. I thought to myself, it's good to be rich once in a while, just to get a new thrill like that. Just the same, I didn't lose my head. Fifty francs! That was quite enough to squander on a rainy night. As I walked off she waved to me with that crazy little bonnet which she didn't know how to wear. It was as though we were old playmates. I felt foolish and giddy. "My dear kind sir . . . you have such a gentle face . . . you are so good, etc." I felt like a saint.

When you feel all puffed up inside it isn't so easy to go to bed right away. You feel as though you ought to atone for such unexpected bursts of goodness. Passing the "Jungle" I caught a glimpse of the dance floor; women with bare backs and ropes of pearls choking them—or so it looked—were wiggling their beautiful bottoms at me. Walked right up to the bar and ordered a *coupe* of champagne. When the music stopped, a beautiful blonde—she looked like a Norwegian—took a seat right beside me. The place wasn't as crowded or as gay as it had appeared from outside. There were only a half dozen couples in the place—they must have all been dancing at once. I ordered another *coupe* of champagne in order not to let my courage dribble away.

When I got up to dance with the blonde there was no one on the floor but us. Any other time I would have been self-conscious, but the champagne and the way she clung to me, the dimmed lights and the solid feeling of security which the few hundred francs gave me, well. . . . We had another dance together, a sort of private exhibition, and then we fell into conversation. She had begun to weep—that was how it started. I thought possibly she had had too much to drink, so I pretended not to be concerned. And meanwhile I was looking around to see if there was any other timber available. But the place was thoroughly deserted.

The thing to do when you're trapped is to breeze—at once. If you don't, you're lost. What retained me, oddly enough, was the thought of paying for a hat check a second time. One always lets himself in for it because of a trifle.

The reason she was weeping, I discovered soon enough, was because she had just buried her child. She wasn't Norwegian either, but French, and a midwife to boot. A chic midwife, I must say, even with the tears running down her face. I asked her if a little drink would help to console her, whereupon she very promptly ordered a whisky and tossed it off in the wink of an eye. "Would you like another?" I suggested gently. She thought she would, she felt so rotten, so terribly dejected. She thought she would like a package of Camels too. "No, wait a minute," she said, "I think I'd rather have *les* Pall Mall." Have what you like, I thought, but stop weeping, for Christ's sake, it gives me the willies. I jerked her to her feet for another dance. On her feet she seemed to be another person. Maybe grief makes one more lecherous, I don't know. I murmured something about breaking away. "Where to?" she said eagerly. "Oh, anywhere. Some quiet place where we can talk."

I went to the toilet and counted the money over again. I hid the hundred franc notes in my fob pocket and kept a fifty franc note and the loose change in my trousers pocket. I went back to the bar determined to talk turkey.

She made it easier for me because she herself introduced the subject. She was in difficulties. It was not only that she had just lost her child, but her mother was home, ill, very ill, and there was the doctor to pay and medicine to be bought, and so on and so forth. I didn't believe a word of it, of course. And since I had to find a hotel for myself, I suggested that she come along with me and stay the night. A little economy there, I thought to myself. But she wouldn't do that. She insisted on going home, said she had an apartment to herself—and besides she had to look after her mother. On reflection I decided that it would be still cheaper sleeping at her place, so I said yes and let's go immediately. Before going, however, I decided it was best to let her know just how I stood, so that there wouldn't be any squawking at the last minute. I thought she was going to faint when I told her how much I had in my pocket. "The likes of it!" she said. Highly insulted she was. I thought there would be a scene. . . . Undaunted, however, I stood my ground. "Very well, then, I'll leave you," I said quietly. "Perhaps I've made a mistake."

"I should say you have!" she exclaimed, but clutching me by the sleeve at the same time: *"Ecoute, chéri . . . sois raisonnable!"* When I heard that all my confidence was restored. I knew that it would be merely a question of promising her a little extra and everything would be O.K. "All right," I said wearily, "I'll be nice to you, you'll see."

"You were lying to me, then?" she said.

"Yes," I smiled, "I was just lying. . . ."

Before I had even put my hat on she had hailed a cab. I heard her give the Boulevard de Clichy for an address. That was more than the price of a room, I thought to myself. Oh, well, there was time yet . . . we'd see. I don't know how it started any more but soon she was raving to me about Henry Bordeaux. I have yet to meet a whore who doesn't know of Henry Bordeaux! But this one was genuinely inspired; her language was beautiful now, so tender, so discerning, that I was debating how much to give her. It seemed to me that I had heard her say— *"quand il n'y aura plus du temps."* It sounded like that, anyway. In the state I was in, a phrase like that was worth a hundred francs. I wondered if it was her own or if she had pulled it from Henry Bordeaux. Little matter. It was Montmartre. "Good evening, mother," I was saying to myself, "daughter and I will look after you—*quand il n'y aura plus de temps!*" She was going to show me her diploma, too, I remembered that.

She was all aflutter, once the door had closed behind us. Distracted. Wringing her hands and striking Sarah Bernhardt poses, half undressed too, and pausing between times to urge me to hurry, to get undressed, to do this and do that. Finally, when she had stripped down and was poking about with a chemise in her hand, searching for her kimono, I caught hold of her and gave her a good squeeze. She had a look of anguish on her face when I released her. "My God! My God! I must go downstairs and have a look at mother!" she exclaimed. "You can take a bath if you like, *chéri*. There! I'll be back in a few minutes." At the door I embraced her again. I was in my underclothes and I had a tremendous erection. Somehow, all this anguish and excitement, all the grief and histrionics, only whetted my appetite. Perhaps she was just going downstairs to quiet her *maquereau*. I had a feeling that something unusual was happening, some sort of drama which I would read about in the morning paper. I gave the place a quick inspection. There were two rooms and a bath, not badly furnished. Rather coquettish. There was her diploma on the wall—"first," as they all read. And there was the photograph of a child, a little girl with beautiful locks, on the dresser. I put the water on for a bath, and then I changed my mind. If something were to happen and I were found in the tub . . . I didn't like the idea. I paced back and forth, getting more and more uneasy as the minutes rolled by.

When she returned she was even more upset than before. "She's going to die . . . she's going to die!" she kept wailing. For a moment I was almost on the point of leaving. How the hell can you climb over a woman when her mother's dying downstairs, perhaps right beneath you? I put my arms around her, half in sympathy and half determined to get what I had come for. As we stood thus she murmured, as if in real distress, her need for the money I had promised her. It was for *"maman."* Shit, I didn't have the heart to haggle about a few francs at the moment. I walked over to the chair where my clothes were lying and I wiggled a hundred franc note out of my fob pocket, carefully keeping my back turned to her just the same. And, as a further precaution, I placed my pants on the side of the bed where I knew I was going to flop. The hundred francs wasn't altogether satisfactory to her but I could see from the feeble way that she protested that it was quite enough. Then, with an energy that astonished me, she flung off her kimono and jumped into bed. As soon as I had put my arms around her and pulled her to me she reached for the switch and out went the lights. She embraced me passionately, and she groaned as all French cunts do when they get you in bed. She was getting me frightfully roused with her carrying on; that business of turning out the lights was a new one to me . . . it seemed like the real thing. But I was suspicious too, and as soon as I could manage conveniently I put my hands out to feel if my trousers were still there on the chair.

I thought we were settled for the night. The bed felt very comfortable, softer than the average hotel bed—and the sheets were clean, I had noticed that. If only she wouldn't squirm so! You would think she hadn't slept with a man for a month. I wanted to stretch it out. I wanted full value for my hundred francs. But she was mumbling all sorts of things in the crazy bed language which goes to your blood even more rapidly when it's in the dark. I was putting up a stiff fight, but it was impossible with her groaning and gasping going on, and her muttering: *"Vite chéri! Vite chéri! Oh, c'est bon! Oh, oh! Vite, vite, chéri!"* I tried to count but it was like a fire alarm going off. *"Vite, chéri!"* and this time she gave such a gasping shudder that bango! I heard the stars chiming and there was my hundred francs gone and the fifty that I had forgotten all about and the lights were on again and with the same alacrity that she had bounced into bed she was bouncing out again and grunting and squealing like an old sow. I lay back and puffed a cigarette, gazing ruefully at my pants the while; they were terribly wrinkled. In a moment she was back again, wrapping the kimono around her, and telling me in that agitated way which was getting on my nerves that I should make myself at home. "I'm going downstairs to see mother," she said. *"Mais faites comme chez vous, chér. Je reviens tout de suite."*

After a quarter of an hour had passed I began to feel thoroughly restless. I went inside and I read through a letter that was lying on the table. It was nothing of any account—a love letter. In the bathroom I examined all the bottles on the shelf; she had everything a woman requires to make herself smell beautiful. I was still hoping that she would come back and give me another fifty francs worth. But time dragged on and there was no sign of her. I began to grow alarmed. Perhaps there *was* someone dying downstairs. Absent-mindedly, out of a sense of self-preservation, I suppose, I began to put my things on. As I was buckling my belt it came to me like a flash how she had stuffed the hundred franc note into her purse. In the excitement of the moment she had thrust the purse in the wardrobe, on the upper shelf. I remembered the gesture she made— standing on her tiptoes and reaching for the shelf. It didn't take me a minute to open the wardrobe and feel around for the purse. It was still there. I opened it hurriedly and saw my hundred franc note lying snugly between the silk coverlets. I put the purse back just as it was, slipped into my coat and shoes, and then I went to the landing and listened intently. I couldn't hear a sound. Where she had gone to, Christ only knows. In a jiffy I was back at the wardrobe and fumbling with her purse. I pocketed the hundred francs and all the loose change besides. Then, closing the door silently, I tiptoed down the stairs and when once I had hit the street I walked just as fast as my legs would carry me. At the Café Boudon I stopped for a bite. The whores were having a gay time pelting a fat man who had fallen asleep over his meal. He was sound asleep; snoring, in fact, and yet his jaws were working away mechanically. The place was in an uproar. There were shouts of "All aboard!" and then a concerted banging of knives and forks. He opened his eyes for a moment, blinked stupidly, and then his head rolled forward again on his chest. I put the hundred franc bill carefully away in my fob pocket and counted the change. The din around me was increasing and I had difficulty to recall exactly whether I had seen "first-class" on her diploma or not. It bothered me. About her mother I didn't give a damn. I hoped she had croaked by now. It would be strange if what she had said were true. Too good to believe. *Vite chéri . . . vite, vite!* And the other half-wit with her "my good sir" and "you have such a kind face!" I wondered if she had really taken a room in that hotel we stopped by.

[1961]

THE CATBIRD SEAT

James Thurber

Mr. Martin bought the pack of Camels on Monday night in the most crowded cigar store on Broadway. It was theatre time and seven or eight men were buying cigarettes. The clerk didn't even glance at Mr. Martin, who put the pack in his overcoat pocket and went out. If any of the staff at F & S had seen him buy the cigarettes, they would have been astonished, for it was generally known that Mr. Martin did not smoke, and never had. No one saw him.

It was just a week to the day since Mr. Martin had decided to rub out Mrs. Ulgine Barrows. The term "rub out" pleased him because it suggested nothing more than the correction of an error—in this case an error of Mr. Fitweiler. Mr. Martin had spent each night of the past week working out his plan and examining it. As he walked home now he went over it again. For the hundredth time he resented the element of imprecision, the margin of guesswork that entered into the business. The project as he had worked it out was casual and bold, the risks were considerable. Something might go wrong anywhere along the line. And therein lay the cunning of his scheme. No one would ever see in it the cautious, painstaking hand of Erwin Martin, head of the filing department at F & S, of whom Mr. Fitweiler had once said, "Man is fallible, but Martin isn't." No one would see his hand, that is, unless it were caught in the act.

Sitting in his apartment, drinking a glass of milk, Mr. Martin reviewed his case against Mrs. Ulgine Barrows, as he had every night for seven nights. He began at the beginning. Her quacking voice and braying laugh had first profaned the halls of F & S on March 7, 1941 (Mr. Martin had a head for dates). Old Roberts, the personnel chief, had introduced her as the newly appointed special advisor to the president of the firm, Mr. Fitweiler. The woman had appalled Mr. Martin instantly, but he hadn't shown it. He had given her his dry hand, a look of studious concentration, and a faint smile. "Well," she had said, looking at the papers on his desk, "are you lifting the oxcart out of the ditch?" As Mr. Martin recalled that moment, over his milk, he squirmed slightly. He must keep his mind on her crimes as a special advisor, not on her peccadillos as a personality. This he found difficult to do, in spite of entering an objection and sustaining it. The faults of the woman as a woman kept chattering on in his mind like an unruly witness. She had, for almost two years now, baited him. In the halls, in the elevator, even in his own office, into which she romped now and then like a circus horse, she was constantly shouting these silly questions at him. "Are you lifting the oxcart out of the ditch? Are you tearing up the pea patch? Are you hollering down the rain barrel? Are you scraping around the bottom of the pickle barrel? Are you sitting in the catbird seat?"

It was Joey Hart, one of Mr. Martin's two assistants, who had explained what the gibberish meant. "She must be a Dodger fan," he had said. "Red Barber announces the Dodger games over the radio and he uses those expressions—picked 'em up down South." Joey had gone on to explain one or two. "Tearing up the pea patch" meant going on a rampage; "sitting in the catbird seat" meant sitting pretty, like a batter with three balls and no strikes on him. Mr. Martin dismissed all this with an effort. It had been annoying, it had driven him near to distraction, but

he was too solid a man to be moved to murder by anything so childish. It was fortunate, he reflected as he passed
on to the important charges against Mrs. Barrows, that he
had stood up under it so well. He had maintained always
an outward appearance of polite tolerance. "Why, I even
believe you like the woman," Miss Paird, his other assis-
tant, had once said to him. He had simply smiled.

A gavel rapped in Mr. Martin's mind and the case
proper was resumed. Mrs. Ulgine Barrows stood charged
with willful, blatant, and persistent attempts to destroy the
efficiency and system of F & S. It was competent, material,
and relevant to review her advent and rise to power. Mr.
Martin had got the story from Miss Paird, who seemed
always able to find things out. According to her, Mrs.
Barrows had met Mr. Fitweiler at a party, where she had
rescued him from the embraces of a powerfully built
drunken man who had mistaken the president of F & S for
a famous retired Middle Western football coach. She had
led him to a sofa and somehow worked upon him a mon-
strous magic. The aging gentleman had jumped to the
conclusion there and then that this was a woman of singular attainments, equipped to bring out the best in him
and in the firm. A week later he had introduced her into
F & S as his special advisor. On that day confusion got its
foot in the door. After Miss Tyson, Mr. Brundage, and
Mr. Bartlett had been fired and Mr. Munson had taken
his hat and stalked out, mailing in his resignation later,
old Roberts had been emboldened to speak to Mr.
Fitweiler. He mentioned that Mr. Munson's department
had been "a little disrupted" and hadn't they perhaps
better resume the old system there? Mr. Fitweiler had
said certainly not. He had the greatest faith in Mrs.
Barrows' ideas. "They require a little seasoning, a little
seasoning, is all," he had added. Mr. Roberts had given

it up. Mr. Martin reviewed in detail all the changes wrought by Mrs. Barrows. She had begun chipping at the cornices of the firm's edifice and now she was swinging at the foundation stones with a pickaxe.

Mr. Martin came now, in his summing up, to the afternoon of Monday, November 2, 1942—just one week ago. On that day, at 3 P.M., Mrs. Barrows had bounced into his office. "Boo!" she had yelled. "Are you scraping the bottom of the pickle barrel?" Mr. Martin had looked at her from under his green eyeshade, saying nothing. She had begun to wander about the office, taking it in with her great, popping eyes. "Do you really need *all* these filing cabinets?" she had demanded suddenly. Mr. Martin's heart had jumped. "Each of these files," he had said, keeping his voice even, "plays an indispensable part in the system of F & S." She had brayed at him, "Well, don't tear up the pea patch!" and gone to the door. From there she had bawled, "But you sure have got a lot of fine scrap in here!" Mr. Martin could no longer doubt that the finger was on his beloved department. Her pickaxe was on the upswing, poised for the first blow. It had not come yet; he had received no blue memo from the enchanted Mr. Fitweiler bearing nonsensical instructions deriving from the obscene woman. But there was no doubt in Mr. Martin's mind that one would be forthcoming. He must act quickly. Already a precious week had gone by. Mr. Martin stood up in his living room, still holding his milk glass. "Gentlemen of the jury," he said to himself, "I demand the death penalty for this horrible person."

The next day Mr. Martin followed his routine, as usual. He polished his glasses more often and once sharpened an already sharp pencil, but not even Miss Paird noticed. Only once did he catch sight of his victim; she swept past him in the hall with a patronizing "Hi!" At five-thirty he walked home, as usual, and had a glass of milk, as usual. He had never drunk anything stronger in his life—unless you could count ginger ale. The late Sam Schlosser, the S of F & S, had praised Mr. Martin at a staff meeting several years before for his temperate habits. "Our most efficient worker neither drinks nor smokes," he had said. "The results speak for themselves." Mr. Fitweiler had sat by, nodding approval.

Mr. Martin was still thinking about that red-letter day as he walked over to the Schrafft's on Fifth Avenue near Forty-sixth Street. He got there, as he always did, at eight o'clock. He finished his dinner and the financial page of the *Sun* at a quarter to nine, as he always did. It was his custom after dinner to take a walk. This time he walked down Fifth Avenue at a casual pace. His gloved hands felt moist and warm, his forehead cold. He transferred the Camels from his overcoat to a jacket pocket. He wondered, as he did so, if they did not represent an unnecessary note of strain. Mrs. Barrows smoked only Luckies. It was his idea to puff a few puffs on a Camel (after the rubbing-out), stub it out in the ashtray holding her lipstick-stained Luckies, and thus drag a small red herring across the trail. Perhaps it was not a good idea. It would take time. He might even choke, too loudly.

Mr. Martin had never seen the house on West Twelfth Street where Mrs. Barrows lived, but he had a clear enough picture of it. Fortunately, she had bragged to everybody about her ducky first-floor apartment in the perfectly darling three-story red-brick. There would be no doorman or other attendants; just the tenants of the second and third floors. As he walked along, Mr. Martin realized that he would get there before nine-thirty. He had considered walking north on Fifth Avenue from Schrafft's to a point from which it would take him until ten o'clock to reach the house. At that hour people were less likely to be coming in or going out. But the procedure would have made an awkward loop in the straight thread of his casualness, and he had abandoned it. It was impossible to figure when people would be entering or leaving the house, anyway. There was a great risk at any hour. If he ran into anybody, he would simply have to place the rubbing-out of Ulgine Barrows in the inactive file forever. The same thing would hold true if there were someone in her apartment. In that case he would say that he had been passing by, recognized her charming house, and thought to drop in.

It was eighteen minutes after nine when Mr. Martin turned into Twelfth Street. A man passed him, a man and a woman, talking. There was no one within fifty paces when he came to the house, halfway down the block. He was up the steps and in the small vestibule in no time, pressing the bell under the card that said "Mrs. Ulgine Barrows." When the clicking in the lock started, he jumped forward against the door. He got inside fast, closing the door behind him. A bulb in a lantern hung from the hall ceiling on a chain seemed to give a mon-strously bright light. There was nobody on the stair, which went up ahead of him along the left wall. A door opened down the hall in the wall on the right. He went toward it swiftly, on tiptoe.

"Well, for God's sake, look who's here!" bawled Mrs. Barrows, and her braying laugh rang out like the report of a shotgun. He rushed past her like a football tackle, bumping her. "Hey, quit shoving!" she said, closing the door behind them. They were in her living room, which ·seemed to Mr. Martin to be lighted by a hundred lamps. "What's after you?" she said. "You're as jumpy as a goat." He found he was unable to speak. His heart was wheezing in his throat. "I—yes," he finally brought out. She was jabbering and laughing as she started to help him off with his coat. "No, no," he said. "I'll put it here." He took it off and put it on a chair near the door. "Your hat and gloves, too," she said. "You're in a lady's house." He put his hat on top of the coat. Mrs. Barrows seemed larger than he had thought. He kept his gloves on. "I was passing by," he said. "I recognized—is there anyone here?" She laughed louder than ever. "No," she said, "we're all alone. You're as white as a sheet, you funny man. Whatever *has* come over you? I'll mix you a toddy." She started toward a door across the room. "Scotch-and-soda be all right? But say, you don't drink, do you?" She turned and gave him her amused look. Mr. Martin pulled himself together. "Scotch-and-soda will be all right," he heard himself say. He could hear her laughing in the kitchen.

Mr. Martin looked quickly around the living room for the weapon. He had counted on finding one there. There were andirons and a poker and something in a corner that looked like an Indian club. None of them would do. It couldn't be that way. He began to pace around. He came to a desk. On it lay a metal paper knife with an ornate handle. Would it be sharp enough? He reached for it and knocked over a small brass jar. Stamps spilled out of it and it fell to the floor with a clatter. "Hey," Mrs. Barrows yelled from the kitchen, "are you tearing up the pea patch?" Mr. Martin gave a strange laugh. Picking up the knife, he tried its point against his left wrist. It was blunt. It wouldn't do.

When Mrs. Barrows reappeared, carrying two highballs, Mr. Martin, standing there with his gloves on, became acutely conscious of the fantasy he had wrought. Cigarettes in his pocket, a drink prepared for him—it was all too grossly improbable. It was more than that; it was impossible. Somewhere in the back of his mind a vague idea stirred, sprouted. "For heaven's sake, take off those gloves," said Mrs. Barrows. "I always wear them in the house," said Mr. Martin. The idea began to bloom, strange and wonderful. She put the glasses on a coffee table in front of a sofa and sat on the sofa. "Come over here, you odd little man," she said. Mr. Martin went over and sat beside her. It was difficult getting a cigarette out of the pack of Camels, but he managed it. She held a match for him, laughing. "Well," she said, handing him his drink, "this is perfectly marvellous. You with a drink and a cigarette."

Mr. Martin puffed, not too awkwardly, and took a gulp of the highball. "I drink and smoke all the time," he said. He clinked his glass against hers. "Here's nuts to that old windbag, Fitweiler," he said, and gulped again. The stuff tasted awful, but he made no grimace. "Really, Mr. Martin," she said, her voice and posture changing, "you are insulting our employer." Mrs. Barrows was now all special advisor to the president. "I am preparing a bomb," said Mr. Martin, "which will blow the old goat higher than hell." He had only had a little of the drink, which was not strong. It couldn't be that. "Do you take dope or something?" Mrs. Barrows asked coldly. "Heroin," said Mr. Martin. "I'll be coked to the gills when I bump that old buzzard off." "Mr. Martin!" she shouted, getting to her feet. "That will be all of this. You must go at once." Mr. Martin took another swallow of his drink. He tapped his cigarette out in the ashtray and put the pack of Camels on the coffee table. Then he got up. She stood glaring at him. He walked over and put on his hat and coat. "Not a word about this," he said, and laid an index finger against his lips. All Mrs. Barrows could bring out was "Really!" Mr. Martin put his hand on the doorknob. "I'm sitting in the catbird seat," he said. He stuck his tongue out at her and left. Nobody saw him go.

Mr. Martin got to his apartment, walking, well before eleven. No one saw him go in. He had two glasses of milk after brushing his teeth, and felt elated. It wasn't tipsiness, because he hadn't been tipsy. Anyway, the walk had worn off all effects of the whiskey. He got in bed and read a magazine for a while. He was asleep before midnight.

Mr. Martin got to the office at eight-thirty the next morning, as usual. At a quarter to nine, Ulgine Barrows, who had never before arrived at work before ten, swept into his office. "I'm reporting to Mr. Fitweiler now!" she shouted. "If he turns you over to the police, it's no more than you deserve!" Mr. Martin gave her a look of shocked surprise. "I beg your pardon?" he said. Mrs. Barrows snorted and bounced out of the room, leaving Miss Paird and Joey Hart staring after her. "What's the matter with that old devil now?" asked Miss Paird. "I have no idea," said Mr. Martin, resuming his work. The other two looked at him and then at each other. Miss Paird got up and went out. She walked slowly past the closed door of Mr. Fitweiler's office. Mrs. Barrows was yelling inside, but she was not braying. Miss Paird could not hear what the woman was saying. She went back to her desk.

Forty-five minutes later, Mrs. Barrows left the president's office and went into her own, shutting the door. It wasn't until half an hour later that Mr. Fitweiler sent for Mr. Martin. The head of the filing department, neat, quiet, attentive, stood in front of the old man's desk. Mr. Fitweiler was pale and nervous. He took his glasses off and twiddled them. He made a small, bruffing sound in his throat. "Martin," he said, "you have been with us more than twenty years." "Twenty-two, sir," said Mr. Martin. "In that time," pursued the president, "your work and your—uh—manner have been exemplary." "I trust so, sir," said Mr. Martin. "I have understood, Martin," said Mr. Fitweiler, "that you have never taken a drink or smoked." "That is correct, sir," said Mr. Martin. "Ah, yes." Mr. Fitweiler polished his glasses. "You may describe what you did after leaving the office yesterday, Martin," he said. Mr. Martin allowed less than a second for his bewildered pause. "Certainly, sir," he said. "I walked home. Then I went to Schrafft's for dinner. Afterward I walked home again. I went to bed early, sir, and read a magazine for a while. I was asleep before eleven." "Ah, yes," said Mr. Fitweiler again. He was silent for a moment, searching for the proper words to say to the head of the filing department. "Mrs. Barrows," he said finally, "Mrs. Barrows has worked hard, Martin, very hard. It grieves me to report that she has suffered a severe breakdown. It has taken the form of a persecution complex accompanied by distressing hallucinations." "I am very sorry, sir," said Mr. Martin. "Mrs. Barrows is under the delusion," continued Mr. Fitweiler, "that you visited her last evening and behaved yourself in an—uh—unseemly manner." He raised his hand to silence Mr. Martin's little pained outcry. "It is the nature of these psychological diseases," Mr. Fitweiler said, "to fix upon the least likely and most innocent party as the—uh—source of persecution. These matters are not for the lay mind to grasp, Martin. I've just had my psychiatrist, Dr. Fitch, on the phone. He would not, of course, commit himself, but he made enough generalizations to substantiate my suspicions. I suggested to Mrs. Barrows, when she had completed her—uh—story to me this morning, that she visit Dr. Fitch, for I suspected a condition at once. She flew, I regret to say, into a rage and demanded—uh—requested that I call you on the carpet. You may not know, Martin, but Mrs. Barrows had planned a reorganization of your department—subject to my approval of course, subject to my approval. This brought you, rather than anyone else, to her mind—but again that is a phenomenon for Dr. Fitch and not for us. So, Martin, I am afraid Mrs. Barrows' usefulness here is at an end." "I am dreadfully sorry, sir," said Mr. Martin.

It was at this point that the door to the office blew open with the suddenness of a gas-main explosion and Mrs. Barrows catapulted through it. "Is the little rat denying it?" she screamed. "He can't get away with that!" Mr. Martin got up and moved discreetly to a point beside Mr. Fitweiler's chair. "You drank and smoked at my apartment," she bawled at Mr. Martin, "and you know it! You called Mr. Fitweiler an old windbag and said you were going to blow him up when you got coked to the gills on your heroin!" She stopped yelling to catch her breath and a new glint came into her popping eyes. "If you weren't such a drab, ordinary little man," she said, "I'd think you'd planned it all. Sticking your tongue out, saying you were sitting in the catbird seat, because you thought no one would believe me when I told it! My God, it's really too perfect!" She brayed loudly and hysterically, and the fury was on her again. She glared at Mr. Fitweiler. "Can't you see how he has tricked us, you old fool? Can't you see his little game?" But Mr. Fitweiler had been surreptitiously pressing all the buttons under the top of his desk and employees of F & S began pouring into the room. "Stockton," said Mr. Fitweiler, "you and Fishbein will take Mrs. Barrows to her home. Mrs. Powell, you will go with them." Stockton, who had played a little football in high school, blocked Mrs. Barrows as she made for Mr. Martin. It took him and Fishbein together to force her out of the doorway into the hall, crowded with stenographers and office boys. She was still screaming imprecations at Mr. Martin, tangled and contradictory imprecations. The hubbub finally died out down the corridor.

"I regret that this has happened," said Mr. Fitweiler. "I shall ask you to dismiss it from your mind, Martin." "Yes, sir," said Mr. Martin, anticipating his chief's "That will be all" by moving to the door. "I will dismiss it." He went out and shut the door and his step was light and quick in the hall. When he entered his department he had slowed down to his customary gait, and he walked quietly across the room to the W20 file, wearing a look of studious concentration.

[1942]

I'VE NEVER HAD IT DONE SO GENTLY BEFORE

For M

Richard Brautigan

The sweet juices of your mouth
are like castles bathed in honey.
I've never had it done so gently before.
You have put a circle of castles
around my penis and you swirl them
like sunlight on the wings of birds.

[1968]

WHEN SMOKE GETS IN YOUR EYES . . . SHUT THEM

Fran Lebowitz

As a practicing member of several oppressed minority groups, I feel that I have on the whole conducted myself with the utmost decorum. I have, without exception, refrained from marching, chanting, appearing on *The David Susskind Show* or in any other way making anything that could even vaguely be construed as a fuss. I call attention to this exemplary behavior not merely to cast myself in a favorable light but also to emphasize the seriousness of the present situation. The present situation that I speak of is the present situation that makes it virtually impossible to smoke a cigarette in public without the risk of fine, imprisonment or having to argue with someone not of my class.

Should the last part of that statement disturb the more egalitarian among you, I hasten to add that I use the word "class" in its narrower sense to refer to that group more commonly thought of as "my kind of people." And while there are a great many requirements for inclusion in my kind of people, chief among them is an absolute hands-off policy when it comes to the subject of smoking.

Smoking is, if not my life, then at least my hobby. I love to smoke. Smoking is fun. Smoking is cool. Smoking is, as far as I am concerned, the entire point of being an adult. It makes growing up genuinely worthwhile. I am quite well aware of the hazards of smoking. Smoking is not a healthful pastime, it is true. Smoking is indeed

no bracing dip in the ocean, no strenuous series of cal-
isthenics, no two laps around the reservoir. On the other
hand, smoking has to its advantage the fact that it is a
quiet pursuit. Smoking is, in effect, a dignified sport.
Not for the smoker the undue fanfare associated with
down-hill skiing, professional football or race-car driving.
And yet, smoking is—as I have stated previously—hazardous. Very hazardous. Smoking, in fact, is downright
dangerous. Most people who smoke will eventually contract a fatal disease and die. But they don't brag about it,
do they? Most people who ski, play professional football
or drive race cars, will not die—at least not in the act—
and yet they are the ones with the glamorous images, the
expensive equipment and the mythic proportions. Why
this should be I cannot say, unless it is simply that the
average American does not know a daredevil when he sees
one. And it is the average American to whom I address
this discourse because it is the average American who is
responsible for the recent spate of no-smoking laws and
antismoking sentiment. That it is the average American
who must take the blame I have no doubt, for unquestion-
ably the *above*-average American has better things to do.

I understand, of course, that many people find smoking
objectionable. That is their right. I would, I assure you, be
the very last to criticize the annoyed. I myself find many—
even most—things objectionable. Being offended is that
natural consequence of leaving one's home. I do not like
after-shave lotion, adults who roller-skate, children who
speak French, or anyone who is unduly tan. I do not,
however, go around enacting legislation and putting up
signs. In private I avoid such people; in public they have
the run of the place. I stay at home as much as possible,
and so should they. When it is necessary, however, to go
out of the house, they must be prepared, as am I, to deal

with the unpleasant personal habits of others. That is what "public" means. If you can't stand the heat, get back in the kitchen.

As many of you may be unaware of the full extent of this private interference in the public sector, I offer the following report:

HOSPITALS

Hospitals are, when it comes to the restriction of smoking, perhaps the worst offenders of all. Not only because the innocent visitor must invariably walk miles to reach a smoking area, but also because a hospital is the singularly most illogical place in the world to ban smoking. A hospital is, after all, just the sort of unsavory and nerve-racking environment that makes smoking really pay off. Not to mention that in a hospital, the most frequent objection of the nonsmoker (that *your* smoke endangers *his* health) is rendered entirely meaningless by the fact that everyone there is already sick. Except the visitor—who is not allowed to smoke.

RESTAURANTS

By and large the sort of restaurant that has "no-smoking tables" is just the sort of restaurant that would most benefit from the dulling of its patrons' palates. At the time of this writing, New York City restaurants are still free of this divisive legislation. Perhaps those in power are aware that if the New Yorker was compelled to deal with just one more factor in deciding on a restaurant, there would be a mass return to home cooking. For there is, without question, at least in my particular circle, not a single person stalwart enough, after a forty-minute phone conversation, when everyone has finally and at long last agreed on Thai food, downtown, at 9:30, to then bear up under the pressures inherent in the very idea of smoking and no-smoking tables.

MINNESOTA

Due to something called the Minnesota Clean Air Act, it is illegal to smoke in the baggage-claim area of the Minneapolis Airport. This particular bit of news is surprising, since it has been my personal observation that even nonsmokers tend to light up while waiting to see if their baggage has accompanied them to their final destination. As I imagine that this law has provoked a rather strong response, I was initially quite puzzled as to why Minnesota would risk alienating what few visitors it had been able to attract. This mystery was cleared up when, after having spent but a single day there, I realized that in Minnesota the Clean Air Act is a tourist attraction. It may not be the Beaubourg, but it's all their own. I found this to be an interesting, subtle concept, and have suggested to state officials that they might further exploit its commercial possibilities by offering for sale plain blue postcards emblazoned with the legend: Downtown Minneapolis.

AIRPLANES

Far be it from me to incite the general public by rashly suggesting that people who smoke are smarter than people who don't. But I should like to point out that I number among my acquaintances not a single nicotine buff who would entertain, for even the briefest moment, the notion that sitting six inches in front of a smoker is in any way healthier than sitting six inches behind him.

TAXICABS

Perhaps one of the most chilling features of New York life is hearing the meter click in a taxicab before one has noticed the sign stating: PLEASE DO NOT SMOKE DRIVER ALLERGIC. One can, of course, exercise the option of dis-embarking immediately should one not mind being out a whole dollar, or one can, more thriftily, occupy oneself instead by attempting to figure out just how it is that a man who cannot find his way from the Pierre Hotel to East Seventy-eighth Street has somehow managed to learn the English word for allergic.

[1977]

ACKNOWLEDGMENTS

AUTHOR BIOGRAPHIES

EVE BABITZ has written articles and stories for *Rolling Stone* and *Esquire*, and is the author of *L.A. Woman* and *Sex and Rage*, among other novels. "Sins of the Green Death" is from *Eve's Hollywood*.

RICHARD BRAUTIGAN was born in Seattle in 1935. He became a comrade of the Beat poets and was the author of *Trout Fishing in America* and *A Confederate General from Big Sur*. By the time of his suicide in 1984, he had completed eighteen books of prose and poetry.

ART BUCHWALD began writing his column for the *New York Herald Tribune* in 1949. He won the Pulitzer Prize in 1982 and his column is now syndicated in nearly five hundred newspapers.

CHARLES BUKOWSKI was born in 1920 and enjoyed an underground reputation for his poetry, short stories, and novels, including *Post Office, Factotum,* and *Ham on Rye*. This excerpt is from his 1978 novel *Women*. He died in 1994.

J. P. DONLEAVY was born in New York City and educated there and at Trinity College in Dublin. His works include *A Singular Man, The Beastly Beatitudes of Balthazar B, The Onion Eaters,* and *The Ginger Man*.

COREY FORD published more than five hundred articles and thirty books. A member of the Algonquin Round Table, he was an early contributor to *The New Yorker* and *Vanity Fair,* and also wrote for the screen. He died in 1969.

SPALDING GRAY is an actor and performance artist best known for autobiographical monologues, including *Terrors of Pleasure, Monster in a Box,* and *Swimming to Cambodia.*

L. RUST HILLS has been the fiction editor of *Esquire* for nearly thirty years. He has published articles and essays and taught writing and literature. "How to Quit Drinking and Smoking Quite So Much" is from his collection *How to Do Things Right: The Memoirs of a Fussy Man.*

ART HOPPE, the sindicated columnist, has written many books and has contributed to *The New Yorker, Harper's, Esquire, Playboy,* and *The Nation.*

ERICA JONG, a poet and novelist, published *Fear of Flying* in 1973. *Ms.* magazine called her the "first woman to write in such a daring and humorous way about sex."

FRAN LEBOWITZ's cynical and sophisticated philosophy has appeared in many magazines as well as her best-selling book *Metropolitan Life.* She has been called "America's #1 chain-smoking, tough-talking headmistress of wit."

DON MARQUIS, novelist, poet, dramatist, and humorist, wrote *The Old Soak* and *Archy and Mehitabel.* "Preface to a Book of Cigarette Papers" was published in the 1919 collection *Prefaces.*

MARY McCARTHY wrote novels, short stories, social and art critisism, and essays. Her books include *Memories of a Catholic Girlhood, The Stones of Florence,* and her best-known novel, *The Group,* excerpted here.

HENRY LOUIS MENCKEN was born in Baltimore in 1880 and died there in 1956. A newspaperman and social critic, he has been called "the great educator of the American people in the significance of their own language." This excerpt first appeared in *The New Yorker* in 1948.

HENRY MILLER is known for the sexual candor of his autobiographical novels, *Tropic of Cancer* and *Tropic of Capricorn*, both long banned in the United States. Born in New York City in 1891, his prolific career spanned nearly five decades. He died in 1980.

VLADIMIR NABOKOV was born in St. Petersburg, Russia, in 1899 and became a United States citizen in 1945. His most popular novels were written in English and include *Lolita* (1959), *Pale Fire* (1962), and *Ada* (1969). He was also a noted lepidopterist.

ANAÏS NIN is best known for her lifelong *Diary*, which she began in 1914. This excerpt is from *Henry and June*, a journal about her relationship with Henry Miller.

DOROTHY PARKER wrote literary and dramatic criticism as well as short stories and verse. She is perhaps best remembered for her fabled wit at the Algonquin Round Table of the 1920s and 1930s.

TOM ROBBINS published the irreverent and whimsical novels *Another Roadside Attraction* and *Even Cowgirls Get the Blues* in the 1970s. This excerpt is from his 1980 novel, *Still Life with Woodpecker*.

ANNE SEXTON, known for her "confessional" verse, won

a Pulitzer Prize for *Live or Die* in 1967. She committed suicide in 1974.

BOB SHACOCHIS (introduction) is a respected libertine and the author of the novel *Swimminmg in the Volcano,* the story collection *Easy in the Islands,* and his newest work, *Domesticity: A Gastronomic Interpretation of Love.*

SAM SHEPARD is a dramatist, poet, and actor whose plays include *Buried Child, Curse of the Starving Class, True West,* and *Fool for Love. Motel Chronicles,* his journal, which was the basis for the film *Paris, Texas,* is excerpted here.

TERRY SOUTHERN has written several novels, including *The Magic Christian, Blue Movie,* and *Flash and Filigree,* as well as screenplays for *Dr. Strangelove, Easy Rider,* and *Barbarella.* MASON HOFFENBERG, under the name of Maxwell Kenton, co-wrote *Candy,* which was first published in France in 1958 and in the U.S. in 1964.

JAMES THURBER was a member of the Algonquin Round Table and was one of the mainstays of *The New Yorker,* where his short stories, essays, and cartoons were published for over thirty years.

MARK TWAIN was the pen name adopted by Samuel Clemens when he was a reporter for the *Virgina City* (Nevada)*Territorial Enterprise.* The celebrated author of *The Adventures of Huckleberry Finn, Tom Sawyer,* and other classics displayed his stinging wit in his essays, letters, and speeches.